LESLIE WEATHERHEAD'S

THE WILL OF GOD

A WORKBOOK

LESLIE WEATHERHEAD'S

THE WILL OF GOD

A WORKBOOK

Rebecca Laird

ABINGDON PRESS
Nashville

Leslie Weatherhead's THE WILL OF GOD
A WORKBOOK

This book is printed on recycled, acid-free paper.

ISBN 0-687-00840-9

05—11

MANUFACTURED IN THE UNITED STATES OF AMERICA

CONTENTS

INTRODUCTION

HOW TO USE THIS WORKBOOK

Tragedy befalls and leaves us confused. Life doesn't turn out as we had planned. World events bring unspeakable horrors into the lives of innocent people. The unimaginable happens and we are left asking, *Why? Why did God let this happen? Why didn't God heal my loved one? Why did God give me these desires and no way to fulfill them?*

When these questions clamor at our hearts we begin to wonder if God is capricious rather than constant, malicious rather than merciful. In times like these, one of the best ways of coming to grips with the great mystery of suffering is to seek to understand God's will. During World War II, when the global community was asking impossible questions while the powers of evil marched through Europe and sailed across the South Pacific shedding blood all along the way, Leslie D. Weatherhead, a British clergyman, preached five sermons on understanding the will of God for the congregation at City Temple in London. These well-reasoned sermons became the classic book *The Will of God*, which has sold more than 800,000 copies in the subsequent fifty years. Weatherhead helps us "get our thinking right about the will of God."

Weatherhead helps us think about how God's will is related to God's character and ultimate intentions for us. As we learn to think first about who God is and what God desires for us, we can better assess and accept the way God is at work in our own lives.

This classic book now is available in workbook form. Key scripture passages, short paragraphs of biblical background information, and key concepts have been added to root the reader in God's ways. Case studies offer true-to-life situations that focus abstract ideas about God's will on specific circumstances in order to help us practice discerning God's will. (These case studies are much like arithmetic problems. Once you begin to understand a concept, the best way to solidify your learning is to apply the concept several times.)

Personal reflection questions and exercises provide tools for delving more deeply into our own perplexing difficulties and core beliefs. Lastly, worship resources give us an opportunity to honor God with our prayers and commitments as we learn.

Guidelines for Personal Use

This workbook is designed to be used by individuals or groups over a period of six weeks. If you are using this workbook on your own during times of personal reflection, it may be best to set aside thirty minutes daily and follow this weekly study pattern:

Day One

Read Weatherhead's chapter and look over the *Purpose of the Lesson*. Pray the *Prayer Before You Begin*. Look up the *Key Scripture* and read the *Scripture Background* and *Key Concepts*. This will orient you to the content you will be learning and applying throughout the week.

Day Two

Read *Case Study #1* and consider the questions.
The first case study each week focuses on a problem faced by an individual.

Day Three

Read *Case Study #2* and consider the questions.
The second case study each week delves into a difficulty that affects a committed relationship.

Day Four

Read *Case Study #3* and consider the questions.
The third case study each week poses a problem that challenges a church community as it seeks to understand God's will.

Day Five

Answer the *Questions for Personal Reflection*.
These questions are to prompt your own reflection. Read all the questions and answer the ones that best stimulate your thinking. It is more important to ponder your own life circumstances than to simply fill in the blank for each question.

Day Six

Do the *Exercises* provided. These exercises will help you put into practice the insights you have gained.

Day Seven

Read the *Reading for Reflection*. Prayerfully remain in God's presence for ten minutes or so. Read aloud the litany, responsive reading, or do the worship activity. Finally pray the benediction and go on with your day in the awareness of God's involvement in your life.

Guidelines for Group Use

If this workbook is used with a group, the leader should encourage each member to follow the above method of personal study during the week. Then, when preparing to lead the group, the *Purpose of the Lesson* will provide the focal point for each weekly session. The *Key Concepts* will serve as the lesson objectives. The leader's goal should be to firmly plant these concepts in each person's understanding by the end of the session. The *Case Studies* will work well in groups of two or three in which each group discusses one of the case studies in depth. The *Worship Resources* will provide structure and worship opportunities.

A one-hour sample group meeting would progress as follows:

The first fifteen minutes

Greet the group and open the session in prayer. Then give the members a chance to check in briefly with the group by saying their name and a sentence or two about how the week is progressing. Read aloud the *Key Scripture* and *Scripture Background*.

The next twenty minutes

Highlight the *Key Concepts* and provide a brief opportunity to discuss each point.

The next fifteen minutes

Divide into small groups and assign one of the *Case Studies* to each group for discussion.

The final ten minutes

Reassemble the entire group and offer a chance for any last questions to be voiced before participating in either the *Litany* or the *Worship Activity*. Have all stand silently as you pray the *Benediction*. Dismiss the group promptly so that those who must leave can do so while others can remain for conversation if desired.

Successful group leaders will adequately prepare, keep the group focused, genuinely care for the participants, and faithfully honor the time commitment made by the participants.

A Guide About Language

The Will of God was written in the early 1940s. Consequently, some words that are considered gender-specific by current standards are used in this text to refer to both men and women.

CHAPTER ONE

GOD'S INTENTIONAL WILL

The phrase "the will of God" is used so loosely, and the consequence of that looseness to our peace of mind is so serious, that I want to spend some time in thinking through with you the whole subject. There is nothing about which we ought to think more clearly; and yet, I sometimes think, there is nothing about which men and women are more confused.

Let me illustrate the confusion. I have a good friend whose dearly loved wife recently died. When she was dead, he said, "Well, I must just accept it. It is the will of God." But he is himself a doctor, and for weeks he had been fighting for her life. He had called in the best specialists in London. He had used all the devices of modern science, all the inventive apparatus by which the energies of nature can be used to fight disease. Was he all that time fighting *against* the will of God? If she had recovered, would he not have called her recovery the will of God? Yet surely we cannot have it both ways. The woman's recovery and the woman's death cannot equally be the will of God in the sense of being his intention.

Let me illustrate the confusion again. "My boy was killed ten days ago in one of the raids on Berlin," said a woman, "but I am trying to bow to the inscrutable will of God." But was that the will of God? I should have said it was the will of the enemy, of Hitler, if you like, of the evil forces we were fighting. Are they then the same thing?

Here is a mother wringing her hands and weeping in anguish because her baby is dead. Her minister stands by her, longing to comfort her; but though his presence and prayers may offer consolation, he knows only too well that when the storm is raging it is too late to talk about the anchor that should have been put down before the storm began. What I mean is that it is so important that we should try to think clearly before disaster falls upon us. If we do, then in spite of all our grief we have a philosophy of life that steadies us as an anchor steadies a ship. If we do not, the storm is so furious that little can be done until it has abated. If only the minister could have injected into the mind of the woman his own belief about God! But that, alas! is impossible. In her anguish, this is what the woman said: "I suppose it is the will of God, *but if only the doctor had come in time he could have saved my baby.*" You see the confusion of thought. If the doctor had come in time, would he have been able to outwit the will of God?

The matter came to me most poignantly when I was in India. I was standing on the veranda of an Indian home darkened by bereavement. My Indian friend had lost his little son, the light of his eyes, in a cholera epidemic. At the far end of the veranda his little daughter, the only remaining child, slept in a cot covered over with a mosquito net. We paced up and down, and I tried in my clumsy way to comfort and console him. But he said, "Well, padre, it is the will of God. That's all there is to it. It is the will of God."

Fortunately I knew him well enough to be able to reply without being misunderstood, and I said something like this: "Supposing someone crept up the steps onto the veranda tonight, while you all slept, and deliberately put a wad of cotton soaked in cholera germ culture over your little girl's mouth as she lay in that cot there on the veranda, what would you think about that?"

"My God," he said, "what would I think about that? Nobody would do such a damnable thing. If he attempted it and I caught him, I would kill him with as little compunction as I would a snake, and throw him over the veranda. What do you mean by suggesting such a thing?"

"But, John," I said quietly, "isn't that just what you have accused God of doing when you said it was his will? Call your little boy's death the result of mass ignorance, call it mass folly, call it mass sin, if you like, call it bad drains or communal carelessness, but don't call it the will of God." Surely we cannot identify as the will of God something for which a man would be locked up in jail, or put in a criminal lunatic asylum.

Those who want a text for this sermon will find it in the eighteenth chapter of St. Matthew's Gospel and the fourteenth verse: "It is NOT the will of your Father which is in heaven, that one of these little ones should perish."

We see by these illustrations—which, of course, could be applied to other disasters besides death—how confused and loose our thinking is about the will of God. But let me here at once relieve the tension of your mind by anticipating some of the things that I want to say in subsequent sermons of this series.

My own thinking demands a division of the subject into three parts, the first of which we are discussing:

1. The intentional will of God.
2. The circumstantial will of God.
3. The ultimate will of God.

The trouble arises because we use the phrase "the will of God" to cover all three, without making any distinction between them. But when we look at the Cross of Christ, we can see, I think, the necessity of such a distinction.

1. Was it God's intention from the beginning that Jesus should go to the Cross? I think the answer to that question must be No. I don't think Jesus thought that at the beginning of his ministry. He came with the *intention* that men should follow him, not kill him. The discipleship of men, not the death of Christ, was the intentional will of God, or, if you like, God's ideal purpose—and I sometimes wish that in common language we could keep the phrase "the will of God" for the intentional will of God.

2. But when circumstances wrought by men's evil set up such a dilemma that Christ was compelled either to die or to run away, then *in those circumstances* the Cross was the will of God, but only in those circumstances which were themselves the fruit of evil. In those circumstances any other way was unworthy and impossible, and it was in this sense that our Lord said, "Nevertheless not what I will, but what thou wilt." Because a father in the evil circumstances set up by war says to his son, "I am glad you are in the Army, John," it does not mean that from the beginning he willed the Army as John's career. The father would much have preferred, let us say, that his son should be an architect. The father wills the Army for his boy only because *in the circumstances which evil has set up* it seems to the father, and, indeed, to the boy, the most honorable, as well as inevitable, thing to do.

3. Then there is a third sense in which we use the phrase "the will of God," when we mean God's ultimate goal—the purposefulness of God which, in spite of evil and, as we shall see, even through evil, arrives, with nothing of value lost, at the same goal as would have been reached if the intentional will of God could have been carried through without frustration. I hope we shall come to see in the other sermons of the series that God cannot be finally defeated, and that is what I mean by his omnipotence—not that everything that happens is his will, but that nothing can happen which *finally* defeats his will. So, in regard to the Cross, God achieved his final goal not simply in spite of the Cross but through it. He achieved a great redemption and realized his ultimate will in as full a sense as he would have done if his intentional will had not been temporarily defeated.

I know people's minds are very tired through war strain and weariness, but I do want to ask you, in view of any possible hour of subsequent sorrow or disaster, to try to hold in your mind those three distinctive ideas which can finally be harmonized, but which, for clarity, we do well to hold separately: the intentional will of God, the circumstantial will of God, and the ultimate will of God.

So we concentrate on the first and think of the will of God in the sense of his ideal intention. To accomplish that, one of the first things we must do is to dissociate from the phrase "the will of God" all that is evil and unpleasant and unhappy. That we shall deal with under the heading "The Circumstantial Will of God." The intentional will of God means the way in which God pours himself out in goodness, such as the true father longs to do for his son.

In this matter see how confused our thinking has been made by bad hymns. Here is a verse from one of them:

Though dark my path and sad my lot,
Let me be still and murmur not,
But breathe the prayer divinely taught,
"Thy will be done."

What sort of a God is this, who of his own *intention*, not through circumstances thrust into life by ignorance, folly, or sin, but of divine intention, pours misery undeserved and unhappiness, disappointment and frustration, bereavement, calamity, and ill health on his beloved children, and then asks them to look up through their tears and say, "Thy will be done"? We simply must break with the idea that everything that happens is the will of God in the sense of being his intention. It is *within* the will of God, if you must use the phrase, in circumstances we have hinted at already. But we must come to terms with the idea that the intentional will of God can be defeated by the will of man *for the time being*. If this were not true, then man would have no real freedom at all. All evil that is temporarily successful temporarily defeats God.

To go back to our earlier illustrations, I could not say to my dear friend, "Your wife's death is not the will of God at all. It is the fruit of human ignorance, and if we could spend as much on medical research as we spend on a battleship, your wife's life could have been saved"; but though it was not the right moment to say it, one could not help thinking it.

When a young missionary declares his readiness and determination, having been thoroughly tested, and having passed all the necessary examinations, to give his life in order to bring the good news about Christ to people who have not heard it, then we may truly say, "Thy will be done." Not when an airman is brought down in flames to meet an untimely death, but when the war is over and the young men of all nations can shake hands and begin together to build a new world—that is the time to say, "Thy will be done." Not when the baby is dead, but when two young people take their little one before the altar to dedicate him or her to God because they want God to be enthroned in their lovely little home and in the new life that has been born to them—that is the time to say, "Thy will be done." Not when little children starve in Europe because of the circumstances of war which the evil of the whole world has brought into being, but when Europe is delivered at last from the ruthless heel of the oppressor, and all little children in a United States of Europe have enough to eat, and can sing and play again happily in the sunshine, with fit bodies and fit minds—that is the time to say, "Thy will be done."

Come with me to some slum home in the dark back streets of a huge city, where men's lives and services are means to other men's ends, where there is disease of body and distortion of mind, where evil festers and grows in sordid and terrible conditions, where men have not even the spirit to rebel, but accept their lot with a listless apathy that is more terrible than a revolution. And if you say concerning those stunted lives, "This is the will of God," I say to you that that is a greater blasphemy than the denial of the Holy Trinity. Industrial oppression, selfish greed, the denial of God's gifts to his own children because of the greed of the few, the horror of war—these things spell a greater atheism than any verbal arguments man has devised. We turn back a hundred years and wonder that Christian men could sing hymns to God while slavery was rife. But, please God, a hundred years hence our descendants will turn back and become incredulous that we ever called ourselves by the name of Christ when his body was torn asunder in our churches, trampled on in our streets, exploited in big business, left to disease when medical knowledge and skill were within reach of the human family, and mutilated by the bombs and burning steel we dropped on one another's cities. Call these things evil, call some of them inevitable evil because of widespread sin, but don't call them the will of God.

Do you not see, therefore, how important it is that we should get our thinking right about the will of God? For by our confusion we thrust people's minds into unbelievable torment; we blunt the edge of social purpose until men mutter the slogan, "God's will be done," when the very opposite of God's will is being done, and when, if men had seen more clearly into the divine purpose and tightened up their loose thinking, they would have become the instruments of God's purpose and swept away the evil which they complacently regarded as the will of God. Men have chanted the phrase "the will of God" as savages chant incantations, sealing the whole subject with that silencing taboo and evading the challenge of the disturbing questions which honest thinking would have set ringing through their minds with the insistence of a trumpet call.

There are, however, two difficulties:

1. The first might be put like this. You may say, "Yes, that's all very well, but people get a lot of comfort from supposing that their tragedies are the will of God. One can bear a thing if it is God's will. It is hard to bear it if it is a ghastly mistake and not the will of God at all. Your view is robbing men of comfort. When they feel a thing is the will of God, they can bear it with equanimity."

I am unrepentant. Admittedly there is a time when things can be said and there is a time when they cannot be said, however true they may be. If you are standing in the presence of some great tragedy, there is very little you can say about the will of God. But I would go on immediately to add this: There is never any final comfort in a lie. However closely we may have hugged a lie to our bosom, the moment we see it to be a lie, we should be wise to part with it. Those who take refuge in a lie are like those who take refuge in a flimsy storm shelter made of three-ply wood painted to look like stone. When they want the shelter most, it will let them down. He who hides in an idea about God which is not true will, in the hour of real need, be left as comfortless as atheism would leave him; and if it is his own refusal to think things through which lands him in a flimsy shelter that can never give his soul any strengthening protection, then the refusal to think is sin, for Christ commanded that we should love him with all our mind. I know that to face the truth is costly, and people hate to be made to think, but only the truth can set us free.

2. Second, there is another objection which could be expressed thus. A man might say, "It is all very well to keep the phrase 'the will of God' for the lovely, joyous, healthy, beneficent things that happen to people; but surely some of the greatest qualities in people are made by suffering, and therefore is not that suffering the will of God? For example," this objector might say, "look how the war brought courage to men and women." This we will discuss more fully as we think of the circumstantial will of God, but let me make some reply to the objection.

15

There is a bad snag in the logic of the objector's remark, for he cannot go on to say, "Therefore the war was the will of God." The war did not *make* courage. It revealed the courage that was there all the time. It gave it a tremendous opportunity for self-expression. Evil is never creative of good, though the circumstances of evil have often been an occasion for the expression of good.

Look not only at the flaw in the logic but at the false implications for theology. If we say that the suffering caused by evil is essential because of the qualities evoked, then logically we must assume that God needs evil to produce good: that he could not produce such a thing as courage unless an evil like war demanded it; that when Jesus healed men he was defying the will of God instead of doing it, in that he was removing something essential to the growth of the soul. If that is true, what happens in the heaven of heavens after all souls are gathered in at last? Will all the qualities which evil reveals atrophy into nothing because there is no evil to evoke them? I repeat that evil does not *make* good qualities. It *reveals* them and gives them exercise, but there is always the possibility—and surely this is God's intention—that those same qualities may be revealed and exercised and manifested as a response to goodness.

Let me recall to you in this connection the words of Jesus: "O Jerusalem, Jerusalem, which killeth the prophets, and stoneth them that are sent unto her! How often would I have gathered thy children together, even as a hen gathereth her chickens under her wings, and ye would not! Behold, your house is left unto you desolate." Note the words "ye would not." They imply, "Ye might have done." Or look at some other words of Jesus: "If thou hadst known in this day . . . the things which belong unto peace! but now they are hid from thine eyes." Note the words "If thou hadst known"; they *might* have known, then. The grand qualities in human nature are not given birth by evil. God creates them, and they are sometimes revealed by the right reaction of the good man to evil, but they do not depend for their origin on evil, for they *can* be evoked by a response to the good.

Let us be very, very careful how we use the phrase "the will of God." I should like in closing this section to make reference to the passing of a very great religious leader, the Rev. Dr. F. Luke Wiseman. On a dreadful, foggy day this old saint of eighty-six preached twice—once in Wesley's own pulpit in City Road. Then the old man made his way home. His wife died many years ago. His family are all grown up. We can imagine the old man sitting down in his armchair by the fire. He went to sleep and awakened in heaven. About that you can use the phrase "Thy will be done"—and some of us would add another Biblical phrase: "May my last end be like his."

We will later fit calamity and distress into the framework of our thought about the will of God, but in the meantime keep the phrase for God's intention. And when you see his glory reflected in this lovely earth, in nature around us so full of his beauty, in poem and song, in picture, in music, in great architecture and in lowly service, in the lives of lovely people, in the happiness of a home, in the health of the body and the resilience of the mind and the saintliness of the soul, then, looking up to your Father in heaven, say, "Thy will be done"; and let us so dedicate ourselves that we may be made one in the glorious harmony of all things and all people who carry out his will, that it may be done in earth as the angels do it in heaven.

CHAPTER ONE
WORKBOOK

GOD'S INTENTIONAL WILL—God's ideal plan for us.

Purpose of the Lesson

To try to think clearly about God's intentional will and purposes for us before difficulties, disaster, or impossible questions befall us. Then, when pain, grief, suffering or confusion come, we will have an understanding of God that will steady us through perplexing times.

A Prayer Before You Begin

Help me, Lord, to understand that you intend all things that are good and right for my life. Teach me more about your purposes and will today.

Key Scripture

"So it is not the will of your Father in heaven that one of these little ones should be lost" (Matthew 18:14).

Scripture Background

This verse is a part of the parable of the lost sheep told by Jesus to illustrate God's desires for the "little ones" or children (also interpreted to mean disciples who are simple and unpretentious in their faith and actions). In this parable Jesus provides an example to those who minister and care for "little ones." Jesus reminds us never to take lightly the loss of a single one of the flock, no matter how insignificant he or she may seem. Through this parable Jesus teaches that God's love is patient, protective, and seeking. God loves each one of the flock and will initiate ways to find and guide the one that has wandered off. We also learn that God rejoices when one who was lost is found.

Key Concepts

- God's intentional will is seen in the way in which God pours out goodness upon us, such as loving parents desire and offer good things for their children.

- The good things in life readily offer us a picture of God's will. God's intentional will is in evidence, "when you see God's glory reflected in this lovely earth, in nature around us so full of beauty, in poem and song, in picture, in music, in great architecture, and in lowly service, in the lives of lovely people, in the happiness of a home, in the health of the body and the resilience of the mind and the saintliness of the soul."

• If we go back to the creation we begin to understand that when God created the world and humankind "God saw everything that he had made, and indeed, it was very good" (Genesis 1:31). From the very beginning God's intentional will for humanity has been whatever is good, pure, and lovely. God's intentional will is that all people become disciples and know of God's love and claim upon our lives.

Read the following case study and consider the questions following it.

CASE STUDY #1   Peter's Story[1]

In a large city a tiny baby was born to a young mother who named him Peter. Soon after delivery, the mother— who had abused intravenous drugs during pregnancy—was diagnosed with AIDS, as was her newborn. The mother took Peter to his grandmother's home.

Several months later the mother died. His grandmother gave him minimal care, offering an occasional bottle and diaper change. Mostly, he was left alone in a crib.

Peter was admitted to the hospital at the age of nine months for "failure to thrive." He weighed less than ten pounds and had little interest in eating. His medical problems were many. He rarely cried. He signaled that he was in need through small whimpers and quiet tears.

The hospital staff filled his barren room with stuffed toys and bright mobiles. Many of the hospital staff came in daily to cuddle him for a few minutes. Thankfully, a minimum of human care and love was afforded to him.

None of his relatives ever returned to take him home.

Considerations

1. What was God's intention for Peter at birth?
2. What was God's intention for Peter's mother? Was contracting AIDS divine punishment for her sins?
3. What or who caused Peter's illness?
4. What role does God play in Peter's suffering?

For further inquiry, look up these scripture verses:

John 9:1-41 (the cause of physical ailments)
2 Corinthians 1:5-11 (suffering and consolation of Christ)
1 Peter 3:17; 4:12-19; 5:10-11 (when Christians suffer)

---

1. This case study is true and used by permission. The names have been changed to protect the privacy of those involved.

Read the following story and consider the questions that follow.

CASE STUDY #2   The Story of Ed and Trina[2]

Ed and Trina met in biology lab in college. Both of them dreamed of being medical missionaries and planned to attend medical school. They came from similar family and church backgrounds. No one questioned the rightness of their marriage. They seem to have been brought together by God. Their wedding was lovely and well attended. Both were accepted into the same medical school in a distant city. They moved, settled in, chose a church to attend, and were soon consumed with the rigors of medical school. Both were challenged by the level of academic work and studied hard. However, when Trina started to struggle with her work, she found a tutor to help her. Ed refused to talk to her or anyone else about his courses. When grades came back after the first semester, Trina did better than Ed. The night after Ed learned that Trina received better grades, he asked her to come home early; she did, expecting they would celebrate surviving their first semester of medical school. However, when she returned home Ed met her at the door with fire in his eyes. He belittled her, they argued, and things escalated until he hit her in a rage.

Trina fled to a friend's house and was devastated. She wondered what had happened to Ed. He had never been violent with her before.

Considerations

1. What was God's intention for Ed?
2. What was God's intention for Trina?
3. What or who caused the marital breakdown?
4. Why didn't God protect Trina from harm?

For further inquiry, look up these scripture verses:

Ephesians 5:22-33 (the mutual submission of marriage)
1 Peter 3:17, 4:12-19, 5:10-11 (when Christians suffer)

---

2. This case study is a fictional story based on composites of several couples known to the author.

Read the following case study and consider the questions that follow.

CASE STUDY #3   The Story of Trinity Church[3]

Trinity Church has an illustrious history. At the turn of the century circuit-riding preachers came to this western town and established a preaching point and Sunday school that drew people from all across the region. The first building was a simple structure, but soon the church grew strong and built a beautiful stone sanctuary with stained-glass windows and row after row of hand-hewn pews. For five decades most of the seats were full and entire families participated. Sadly, for the last twenty years the congregation has dwindled. The neighborhood changed as businesses moved away from the downtown area. Many parishioners moved to larger homes in the newly built subdivisions. Most of the old homes near the church were converted into multiple-family dwellings and most of those who lived in the area were financially strapped. Many were new immigrants who hoped the area's rapid growth and agricultural base would provide jobs.

Considerations

1. What was God's intention for Trinity Church?
2. What was God's intention for the people who live near the church?
3. What or who caused the decline in church attendance?
4. What role does God play in the rise or decline, the past and future of Trinity Church or any church?

For further inquiry, look up these scripture verses:

Matthew 25:34-40 (caring for the least of these)
Matthew 28:18-20 (Jesus' commission to the disciples)
Ephesians 3:14-20, 4:11-16 (nature and function of the church)
1 Corinthians 12:24b-26 (when one suffers, all suffer)

---

3. This case study is a composite drawn from several churches known to the author.

Questions for Personal Reflection

1. If God's intentional will is seen in the way God pours out goodness upon us, much as parents give good gifts and offer care to their children, how has God shown goodness to you?

2. Recall a time when someone you love suffered. How did you respond? How has God responded to you in times of suffering?

3. Have you ever been baffled or confused about God's will? What were the circumstancces? In retrospect, can you learn anything about God's intention for your life in this particular circumstance?

4. In the first chapter Weatherhead tells us that to wrongly attribute suffering to God's will is like hugging a lie to our bosom. The one "who hides in an idea about God which is not true will, in the hour of real need, be left comfortless." Have you ever believed something about God's will for you that later proved to be untrue or left you adrift? Have your beliefs changed? What do you now believe?

5. Weatherhead writes, "Evil does not *make* good qualities. It *reveals* them and gives them exercise, but there is always the possibility—and surely this is God's intention— that those same qualities may be revealed and exercised and manifested as a response to goodness." During adversity what qualities surfaced in you or in someone you have known? How can you put those qualities to work today?

6. Suppose a friend calls you today with tragic news: perhaps she has suffered a miscarriage or he has been diagnosed with prostate cancer. Your friend asks, "Is it God's will that I suffer so?" How will you respond?

Exercises

1. In the following space draw a sidewalk, with each block representing a major event in your life. Write short descriptions inside each block (marriage to Joe, birth of daughter, death of mother, house fire, etc.) Beside each block write short descriptive phrases about what God intended for you each step along the way. (Marriage provided companionship and love, daughter taught me patience, death reminded me that relationships transcend death, fire helped me refocus on importance of life rather than material things, etc.) Look at the entire sidewalk. Whatever the circumstances of your life, God's desire has been that good befall you throughout your life.

2. Read the headlines of today's newspaper. In the left-hand column below write down three headlines that deal specifically with tragedy. In the middle column write down God's intention for those involved in the story. In the right-hand column write down one specific thing you can pray for regarding that specific situation. Then pray.

TODAY'S HEADLINE	GOD'S INTENTION	PRAYER REQUEST

Worship Resources

Reading for Reflection

If we want to understand God's goodness in his gifts, then we must think of them as a responsibility we bear for our brothers [and sisters]. Let no one say: "God has blessed me with money and possessions, and then live as if he and his God were alone in the world. For the time will come when he realizes that he has been worshiping the idols of his good fortune and selfishness. Possessions are not God's blessing and goodness, but the opportunities of service which he entrusts to us."[4]

Dietrich Bonhoeffer

Litany

When suffering touches my life,
Help me, O God to pray, *Thy will be done.*

When I wonder at your purposes and ways,
Help me, O God to pray, *Thy will be done.*

When I stray and wander away,
Help me, O God to pray, *Thy will be done.*

When I see your glory in loving people,
Help me, O God to pray, *Thy will be done.*

When great music restores my soul,
Help me, O God to pray, *Thy will be done.*

When your presence attends me,
Help me, O God to pray, *Thy will be done.*

Benediction

"Let us so dedicate ourselves that we may be made one in the glorious harmony of all things and all people who carry out God's will, that it may be done on earth as the angels do it in heaven." Amen.

---

4. Dietrich Bonhoeffer, "God's Loving Care and Human Suffering," in *A Testament to Freedom: The Essential Writings of Dietrich Bonhoeffer*, eds. Geffrey B. Kelly and F. Burton Nelson (San Francisco: Harper and Row, 1990), 207.

CHAPTER
TWO

GOD'S CIRCUMSTANTIAL WILL

We said that the phrase "the will of God" is used so loosely as to land us not only in a confusion of mind but in a torment of feeling.

When a dear one dies, we call it "the will of God," though the measures we used to prevent death could hardly be called fighting against the will of God, and if they had been successful we should have thanked God with deep feeling that in the recovery of that dear one his will had been done. Similarly, when sadness, disease, and calamity overtake men they sometimes say with resignation, "God's will be done," when the opposite of his will has been done. When Jesus healed men's bodies and gladdened men's lives in Palestine, he was doing the will of God, not undoing or defeating it.

We therefore divided our subject into three as follows:

1. The intentional will of God—God's ideal plan for men.
2. The circumstantial will of God—God's plan within certain circumstances.
3. The ultimate will of God—God's final realization of his purposes.

Once again, even at the risk of being tiresome, let us look at the supreme illustration of the Cross.

1. It was not the intentional will of God, surely, that Jesus should be crucified, but that he should be followed. If the nation had understood and received his message, repented of its sins, and realized his kingdom, the history of the world would have been very different. Those who say that the Crucifixion was the will of God should remember that it was the will of evil men.

2. But when Jesus was faced with circumstances brought about by evil and was thrust into the dilemma of running away or of being crucified, then *in those circumstances* the Cross was his Father's will. It was in this sense that Jesus said, "Not what I will, but what thou wilt."

3. The ultimate will of God means, in the case of the Cross, that the high goal of man's redemption or, to use simpler English, man's recovery to a unity with God—a goal which would have been reached by God's intentional plan had it not been frustrated—will still be reached through his circumstantial will. In a sentence, no evil is finally able to defeat God or to cause any "value" to be lost.

Let us now concentrate on the second of these divisions and speak about what I call "the circumstantial will of God." We may make the matter clearer still by restating an earlier illustration and thinking of a father planning his boy's career, in co-operation with the boy himself. The will of both may have been, let us say, that the boy should become an architect. Then comes the war. The father is quite willing for his son to be in the armed forces; but a Navy, Army, or Air Force career is only the father's interim or circumstantial will for his boy, his will in the circumstances of evil which war has produced. It would only be confusing to speak as if the father's ideal intention and original plan for his son was that the latter should spend valuable years of his life in the armed forces.

Now in the same way there is an intentional purpose of God for every man's life; but because of human folly and sin, because man's free will creates circumstances of evil that cut across God's plans, because our oneness with the great human family means that the evil among other members of it may create circumstances which disturb God's intention for us, there is a will within the will of God, or what I call "the circumstantial will of God"; and in the doing of that the soul can find peace, the mind can find poise, and the will can be so expressed that ultimately the original plan of God is brought to successful fruition.

I think there are two parts to the circumstantial will of God—one in the natural realm and the other in the spiritual.

1. Let us look at the Cross of Christ again. Given the circumstances of evil, it was God's will that Jesus should be betrayed, taken, crowned with thorns, crucified, left there in the blazing sun to die. The laws of the universe, which are themselves an expression of God's will, were not set aside for Jesus, the beloved Son. The laws which govern the hammering in of nails held on the day of Crucifixion in just the same way as they do when you nail up a wooden box. If bombs are dropped from an airplane over the closely built dwellings in a city, they pierce the roofs of the godly and of the ungodly; and if nails are hit with a hammer wielded by a strong arm, they pierce the flesh even of the Son of God; and because the laws of the universe are operating, and because those laws are an expression of God's will, you may, if you like, call these things the will of God, but only in the limited sense described. The forces of nature carry out their functions and are not deflected when they are used by the forces of evil. Those who lost dear ones in recent wars will not need me to say more about that. When Christ's flesh was lacerated on the cross, the laws of God in regard to pain operated just as they do when we get hurt; and Christ accepted that as part of the ordering of the universe which was the will of a

wise, holy, and loving God. He did not fling it back at God that it was unfair that the laws should operate in his case because of his character.

2. But there is a second element within that circumstantial will of God. The first we may call natural, the second spiritual. Christ did not just submit to this dread event of the Crucifixion with what we miscall "resignation." He took hold of the situation. Given those circumstances which evil had produced, it was also God's will that Jesus should not just die like a trapped animal, but that he should so react to evil, positively and creatively, as to wrest good out of evil circumstances; and that is why the Cross is not just a symbol of capital punishment similar to the hangman's rope, but is a symbol of the triumphant use of evil in the cause of the holy purposes of God. In other words, by doing the circumstantial will of God we open up the way to God's ultimate triumph with no loss of anything of value to ourselves.

Now let us turn from the Cross and see this truth in a very human illustration. Take the case of the unmarried woman in middle life whose mind has almost closed against the probability of marriage. What was once an eager expectancy becomes a hope growing dimmer and dimmer, and then dying away. Now it is not the intentional will of God that she should remain unmarried. The divine intention, surely, is that every woman should have a home and a husband and babies. The very structure of her body and the creative centers in her brain, her sex instinct and her maternal impulse, are sufficient evidence of this, for every woman possesses all these things. Though some instincts can be repressed into unconsciousness, or can be diverted into nonbiological activities, every instinct is present in every person, and biological fulfillment is God's intentional plan.

But supposing that the tyranny of evil circumstances—and they are evil if they deprive women of their primary *raison d'être*—thrusts a woman into a dilemma. She cannot have that part of her nature biologically satisfied, let us imagine, unless she sacrifices her ideals—cannot have sex without sin. Then the circumstantial will of God is that she shall remain frustrated, and that circumstantial will can be looked at from two angles. It falls into two parts—one natural, the other spiritual.

First, there will be a physical sense of sex starvation, for no so-called sublimation completely solves the difficulty here. Sublimation is always a second-best for the time being. But, second, she must not merely resign herself, perhaps with bitterness, to the unmarried state, but must react so creatively and positively to God's circumstantial will that she makes something glorious out of life which God can use for the fulfillment of his ultimate will, namely, to make her a complete and integrated personality in union with himself.

We note, then, that the second part of God's circumstantial will cannot be done without human co-operation. Without that, the Cross would have been another in the long list of capital sentences carried out by a savage and barbarous state. It would have been a noble sacrifice for an ideal. In the case of the kind of woman we have described, without cooperation the woman would simply resign herself to the forces of the universe and make her frustration unendurable. She has to find by a positive and creative attitude to the situation—which, be it noted, evil, not God, has thrust upon her—the circumstantial will of God in it, so that out of the frustration she may make an immense contribution both to her own inner harmony and to the final purposes of God. This, in fact, is what many women have done. Sublimation is easier to talk about than to accomplish. It is particularly easy for those who do not have to practice it to talk about its value for others. Actually, it is not technically sublimation until it becomes unconscious—until, that is to say, our instinctive energies are running in a nonbiological channel without our realizing the fact at all. But sublimation may well begin by directing the activities of the personality to some altruistic task which is (*a*) of use to the community, (*b*) satisfying to the self, and (*c*) in harmony with that self's ideals. Only under those three conditions can effective sublimation be realized.

The common illustration is work among other people's children. But in doctoring, nursing, craftsmanship, music, writing, organizing, running clubs and other people's homes, women use up the energy in ways helpful to the community, satisfying to themselves, in harmony with their ideals; and in so doing they extend immensely the kingdom of God.

In parenthesis, one ought to add that nothing could be more cruel or heartless or stupid than to sneer at the unmarried woman in middle life. It is especially intolerable when such a sneer comes from those who are married for no reason for which they should be proud. All who work among the people will report that wherever unselfish service for others is being carried on at a sacrifice of personal comfort, there the unmarried woman in middle life will be found, serving the community and forcing the circumstances of evil that have frustrated God's intentional will to contribute to the achievement of his ultimate plan.

I can imagine such a woman saying, "I know that the will of God was that I should express my nature as other happily married women do, and of course I should love to have my own home and family. But I am not just going to let the universe get me down, for there are no circumstances which God allows that can finally defeat the ultimate purpose which he wills; and as Jesus reacted to the circumstances of evil and thereby turned his crown of thorns into a crown of glory, and his cross into a throne, I can take hold of these circumstances and win something from them that will bring harmony to my own nature, which will contribute to the happiness and service of the world, and which will further the kingdom of God."

No one, you see, can say to God: "Well, of course I wanted to do this and that, but I was the victim of illness or sorrow or frustration or war or death or loss. So what could I do?" For there are no circumstances which will be so deadly as those Christ had to face. No possible situation can ever arise which *of itself* has the power either to down us or to defeat God—no, not even death. For although thousands of deaths happen that are not the intentional will of God, he is not beaten by any possible juxtaposition of circumstance. Probably death, and therefore the fact that we serve him in heaven instead of on earth, does not make more difference to the ultimate plans of God than whether we serve him in London or Manchester.

One thing *is* incredible, that God should allow circumstances to happen which inevitably defeat his ultimate purposes. If he did, it would mean that he had abdicated from the throne of the universe, whereas the truth is that, though the revolt against him seems formidable, "the Lord God omnipotent reigneth." As the writer to the Hebrews said, "We see not yet all things subjected to him. But we behold him . . . crowned with glory and honour."

So, to go back to our early illustrations of death which we too loosely called "the will of God," we can only admit them as God's circumstantial will. Somebody once asked me, when a baby had fallen out of a fifth-story window, whether its death was the will of God. The question shows how important it is that we should get our thinking straight, for the answer is both Yes and No. Yes, it is God's circumstantial will. I mean there that it is God's will that the law of gravity should operate. It is God's will that a baby is made of flesh and blood; and if a baby hits a concrete pavement after falling from such a height, of course it is God's will that the little body should be broken—otherwise God would have made babies' bodies of something like India rubber. Yet we feel that we must answer the question by an emphatic No and say that the death of the baby was not the will of God, for it was not the will of God that it should be allowed to fall out of the window at all.

Again and again, when people ask, "Is it the will of God?" I think we shall have to separate the subject in order to make an intelligent answer.

Consider, for example, the matter of disease. The Christian minister is continually confronted, as he does his visiting, by the question as to whether the onset of disease is the will of God. The important answer is No. The will of God for man is perfect health. Other things being equal, God can use a body free from disease more effectively than a diseased body. Jesus would not have been a greater spiritual asset in his early ministry if he had been lame or diabetic or tubercular. But there is a will of God within evil circumstances; and let every sufferer who may happen to read these lines realize that if he makes the right reaction to these circumstances, the ultimate will of God will be reached *as effectively as if he had not been ill.* God would not allow cancer if *of itself* it had the power to defeat him.

The point may be seen, perhaps, by thinking of those diseases which are due to an invasion of germs. I suppose God is responsible for the creation of germs, even the germs of disease. Why they are created I don't know. It may be that they serve some good function about which we know nothing. It may be that they have served, in the evolutionary process, some good function. I don't think anybody knows the answer to that question. If these germs invade a body the resistance of which evil circumstances have lowered, then the result is disease; and that disease you can call, if you like, the circumstantial will of God. But it is the will of God only within the circumstances created by evil.

Here again let me repeat that that circumstantial will can be viewed from two angles—the first natural, the second spiritual. There is the physical condition which we call disease; but, second, there is the possibility of the patient's making such a splendid response to that circumstance that he creates out of it a spiritual asset in the community of much more value than most people's health. It is because the saints have thus reacted to evil that the fallacy has got about that disease and suffering are the will of God. Let me put it this way. Given a spiritual awakening so glorious that the personality lives in close co-operation with God, the healthy body is more in line with his will. But so many healthy people are spiritually asleep and are not co-operating with him at all, and so many sick people have, through the sickness, become spiritually awakened during their illness that out of the circumstances of evil they have created and set free spiritual energies far more valuable than the spiritual apathy of the healthy person.

I am quite sure that the battle *against* disease is the will of God, and I thank God for all those people who are taking part in it. In olden days in this country, wolves used to descend from the woods upon a village and do a great deal of harm. But our sturdy forefathers did not call the invasion of the wolves "the will of God." They called up all their resources, and they "liquidated" the wolves. When the community is set upon by an invasion of germs, that is not the will of God. The situation is just the same. You may tell me that the animals are smaller and the germs of disease can be seen only through a microscope, but the problem is the same, and the battle is the same. I cannot understand how anybody who has read the New Testament can ever stand at the bedside of a patient and, without explaining himself, utter the pathetic complaint that disease is the will of God. I always imagine that Jesus would speak with anger about such a thoughtless dictum. When a woman was brought to him who had been ill for a long time, he spoke of her as "this woman . . . whom Satan hath bound, lo, these eighteen years." Satan! As far as I can understand Jesus' attitude, both in the words he spoke and the healing miracles he so gloriously wrought, he always regarded disease as part of the kingdom of evil, and with all his powers he fought it and instructed his followers to do the same.

I like to think of our Lord standing by the bedside of the patient and working with the doctors and nurses toward the regaining of health, working on the mind and spirit of the patient as the physicians work on the body. Then, if the latter fail, I like to think of him showing the sufferer that, in co-operation with him, victory may still be wrested from defeat and the purposes of God realized.

One final thought. If you say, "Well, it's a bit casual of God to *allow* these things to happen if they are not his intention," I agree that there is mystery there. It would be foolish to speak as if all the ways of God to men were clear. I should not like to give the impression that I could make a glib answer to any specific case of suffering that was brought to my notice. I too am often appalled at the suffering people endure, and especially little children.

Yet I wonder if, in a sense, we are not all in the position of little children. I can imagine a child looking up to his own father who loves him, and saying to him, "Don't you think you are rather casual to let me get hurt the way you do?" I amused myself, as I thought about this, by imagining a mass meeting of tiny toddlers who magically had the gift of putting their thoughts into words. Think of them, if you like, crowded into a great hall, with a little toddler as chairman, who, adjusting his bib, addresses his fellow toddlers in some such way as this: "I am sure my parents don't care. Look at my knees!" And there they were all red and scratched. And I imagined the meeting passing this resolution: "That this meeting protests against the carelessness of parents, and demands that in future no furniture shall be made with sharp corners, that gravel paths and hard playgrounds shall be abolished, and that claws shall be removed from the paws of all tame cats." I am sure the resolution would be passed unanimously. We do not say to God, "Look at my knees!" but we do say, "Look at my frustration and sorrow and disappointment and pain! How *can* you be so callous, and how *do* you expect us to think you care?" Perhaps childhood's tragedies are to us what our tragedies are to God—not that he is callous any more than the ideal parent is, but that his perspective is different. But the thought that comforts the child comforts me. If the child thought about it, I think he would say, "There is much I don't understand, but I know that my father both loves and cares." So, for myself, I am quite certain that because God is love there is nothing in his world that can be regarded as meaningless torture. There is much I cannot understand. There must be much that I cannot be made to understand until I have passed out of childhood's stage. But because I know him through other means, and especially as revealed in Jesus, I know that although I cannot understand the answer to my questions, there *is* an answer, and in that I can rest content.

> I only know I cannot drift
> Beyond His love and care.

One cannot avoid being deeply impressed by the kind of answer Jesus gave when men came to him with their questions. When John the Baptist asked him a question, he said, "Suffer it to be so now." When Peter asked him a question, he said, "What I do thou knowest not now; but thou shalt know hereafter." And when, on the darkest night of the world's history, the night before his death, they all asked him questions, he said, "I have yet many things to say unto you, but ye cannot bear them now."

You see, even Jesus did not say, "I have explained the world." What he did say was, "I have overcome the world." And if we can only trust where we cannot see, walking in the light we have—which is often very much like hanging on in the dark—if we do faithfully that which we see to be the will of God in the circumstances which evil thrusts upon us, we can rest our minds in the assurance that circumstances which God allows, reacted to in faith and trust and courage, can never defeat purposes which God ultimately wills. So doing, we shall wrest from life something big and splendid. We shall find peace in our own hearts. We shall achieve integration in our own minds. We shall be able to serve our fellows with courage and joy. And then one day—for this has been promised us—we shall look up into his face and understand. Now we see in a mirror, darkly, but then face to face. Frankly, hard though it be to say so, it is a lack of faith not to be able to bear the thought of anything which God allows.

> I know that right is right; that givers shall increase;
> That duty lights the way for the beautiful feet of peace;
> That courage is better than fear, and faith is truer than doubt.
> And fierce though the fiends may fight, and long though the angels hide,
> I know that Truth and Right have the Universe on their side;
> And that somewhere beyond the stars is a Love that is stronger than hate;
> When the night unlocks her bars, I shall see Him—and I will wait.

CHAPTER TWO
WORKBOOK

GOD'S CIRCUMSTANTIAL WILL—God's plan and provision within
certain circumstances and conditions.

Purpose of the Lesson

To understand that human folly and sin often delay or prevent God's intentional will from coming to fruition in our lives. Thus in the circumstances created by evil or neglect, there is a "will within the will of God." This means that God will make provision to help us overcome and bring good out of current circumstances.

A Prayer Before You Begin

O God, I confess that there is much I don't understand about the circumstances of my life, yet today I affirm my belief that you love and care for me and the world in which I live.

Key Scripture

"And [Jesus] said to them, 'I am deeply grieved, even to death; remain here, and keep awake.' And going a little farther, he threw himself on the ground and prayed that, if it were possible, the hour might pass from him. He said, 'Abba, Father, for you all things are possible; remove this cup from me; yet not what I want, but what you want' " (Mark 14:34-36).

Scripture Background

This story gives us a glimpse into the humanity of Jesus. He did not wish to die and he knew that suffering awaited him. He did not fully understand why this had to happen. Faith in God's ultimate control was required of Jesus. Jesus had to accept and follow God's leading although many things remained a mystery. Jesus poured out his desires to God, knowing that God was his Abba—his loving parent who wished goodness for him. Then, ultimately he submitted to the will of God—not with desolation or self-pity, but with the commitment to live as God's chosen one, no matter what the cost. When Judas and the soldiers arrived to arrest him he did not run nor bargain for his life. He faced the path he had accepted as God's will and walked forward with faith.

Key Concepts

• In the particular circumstances of life, God's will for us has two sides: (1) to accept that we are subject to the divinely ordered natural laws of the universe; and (2) to actively respond to evil, positively and creatively, as to wrest good out of evil circumstances. By so doing we open the way to God's ultimate triumph.

• God has ordered the natural realm. God ordains that universal laws remain in place, even when human violation of natural law results in suffering and death. When a hammer strikes flesh it bruises, bloodies and hurts. Jesus suffered physical pain just as did the two thieves on either side of him. No one (barring a miracle) is exempt from the natural results of universal laws. Using a current example, if bombs are mistakenly dropped over closely built dwellings in Bosnia, they shatter the roofs of the godly and ungodly alike. One of the universal laws is that sin exacts a wage. And we suffer not just from the consequences of our own sins, but from the sins of others. There is a oneness within the great human family. Evil among other members of it may create circumstances which disturb God's intention for us.

• God is at work and we also can participate in the outcome of events by our choices. Jesus reacted to evil, positively and creatively, as to wrest good out of evil circumstances and made the cross a symbol of the triumphant use of evil in the cause of the holy purposes of God. Jesus loved even on the cross and that opened the way for God to raise him from the dead as victor over sin and death. This second means of finding God's provision and redemption in God's circumstantial will requires human cooperation. We know that we are choosing cooperation with God's circumstantial will when we react to suffering and tragedy in ways that are consistent with the following:

  * our actions are of use to the community or they benefit the common good of humankind.
  * our actions or attitudes are satisfying a true God-given need.
  * our actions and attitudes are in harmony with personal and spiritual values.

Read the following case study and consider the questions that follow.

CASE STUDY #1   **Peter's Story**

While in the hospital, Peter, a nine-month-old baby with AIDS, becomes a ward of the state. A foster mother is contacted to consider taking him into her home. She currently is the foster mother to another infant. This woman formerly was a nurse on the AIDS ward of an urban hospital. She certainly has the skills to care for Peter, but can she handle two infants with special needs on her own? The stipend for foster care is modest. Can she make it financially? She seeks the wisdom of friends, fellow church members, doctors and parents of other children with HIV/AIDS. The advice she receives is divided. Many fear she is taking on too much. Others remind her that she became a foster mother precisely with the idea in mind of providing a home for AIDS-affected children.

Considerations

1. Weatherhead points out that "because of our oneness with the great human family . . . evil among other members of it may create circumstances which disturb God's intention for us." How has this "oneness" influenced Peter's life both negatively and positively?

2. What natural laws are in effect in Peter's life? Natural laws of the universe continue to operate despite abuses of human freedom, and are not broken by God (except through miracles) to save us from suffering. In the book *The Will of God* it states: If "germs invade a body the resistance of which evil circumstance have lowered, the result is disease." In other words, germs and viruses cause disease. If our bodies come in contact with them and our immune systems are weak [in this case through drug abuse] then we will be infected—that is a natural law.

3. Does God overrule natural laws and provide miracles? What would be a miracle in this situation? Do you believe one could happen?

4. Regarding Peter's life, how can we understand the circumstantial will of God in the spiritual realm? How could others cooperate with God to wrest good out of the evil that has befallen Peter?

5. How do these acts of cooperation meet Weatherhead's guidelines?
    * actions are of use to the community or benefit the common good of humankind.
    * actions or attitudes are satisfying a true need.
    * actions and attitudes are in harmony with personal and spiritual values.

For further inquiry, look up these scripture verses:

Micah 6:8-9 (God's requirements of us)

Mark 3:31-35 (Jesus defines the spiritual nature of family)

Psalm 68:5-6 (In God's circumstantial will, an extended family is provided to care for orphans, the sick, and the lonely)

Read the following case study and consider the questions that follow.

CASE STUDY #2   The Story of Ed and Trina

After a violent domestic episode that followed the completions of the first semester of medical school, Trina moves away from her husband, Ed. They live apart for a few months and together see a counselor. Trina learns that Ed's father occasionally beat his mother—this is news to her after all these years of knowing him. Ed doesn't think his background or one violent episode determines that he will repeatedly harm his wife. They agree to try again, but after a few months Ed gets violent again—this time after his research funding isn't renewed. Ed doesn't physically hurt Trina but he burns her class notes in the fireplace and breaks household objects. Trina moves out again. She lives by herself and transfers to another medical school an hour away, so that she and Ed won't be in situations that might make Ed feel that she is competing with him. She vows to continue to fulfill her calling but wonders what is God's will for her marriage in these terrible days.

Considerations

1. Weatherhead points out that "because of our oneness with the great human family . . . evil among other members of it may create circumstances which disturb God's intention for us." How has this "oneness" influenced Ed's and Trina's lives both negatively and positively?

2. What natural laws are in effect in the lives of this couple? Natural laws of the universe continue to operate despite abuses of human freedom, and are not broken by God (except through miracles) to save us from suffering.

3. Does God overrule natural laws and provide miracles? What would be a miracle in this situation? Do you believe one could happen?

4. Regarding Ed and Trina, how can we understand the circumstantial will of God in the spiritual realm? How could these two cooperate with God to wrest good out of the evil that has befallen them?

5. How do these acts of cooperation meet Weatherhead's guidelines?
   * actions are of use to the community or benefit the common good of humankind.
   * actions or attitudes are satisfying a true need.
   * actions and attitudes are in harmony with personal and spiritual values.

For further inquiry, look up these scripture verses:

Micah 6:8-9 (God's requirements of us)
Matthew 7:21-23 (the eternal importance of doing the will of God)
John 7:16-18 (characteristics of one who seeks God's will)

Read the following case study and consider the questions that follow.

CASE STUDY #3   **Trinity Church**

After a period of decline in membership, the leadership of Trinity Church splits down the middle. One group wants to relocate outside the inner city while the other wants to stay put and refocus the resources of the church on the people who live near the existing building. Several influential families leave; the rest are determined to band together and pray for guidance. The remaining few decide to open a day care center as an outreach ministry to low-income and working class families. A few new families from the neighborhood begin to attend and take leadership in the outreach efforts of the church, but financial problems continue to plague the church and threaten its closure.

Considerations

1. Weatherhead points out that "because of our oneness with the great human family . . . evil among other members of it may create circumstances which disturb God's intention for us." How has this "oneness" influenced Trinity Church negatively and positively?

2. What natural laws are in effect in the life of this church? Natural laws of the universe continue to operate despite abuses of human freedom, and are not broken by God (except through miracles) to save us from suffering.

3. Does God overrule natural laws and provide miracles? What would be a miracle in this situation? Do you believe one could happen?

4. Regarding Trinity Church, how can we understand the circumstantial will of God in the spiritual realm? How could the church members cooperate with God to wrest good out of the evil that has befallen them?

5. How do these acts of cooperation meet Weatherhead's guidelines?
   * actions are of use to the community or benefit the common good of humankind.
   * actions or attitudes are satisfying a true need.
   * actions and attitudes are in harmony with personal and spiritual values.

For further inquiry, look up these scripture verses:

Micah 6:8-9 (God's requirements of us)
Hebrews 10:32-39 (Persevering in doing God's will)

Questions for Personal Reflection

1. How has the "oneness with the great human family" and the "evil among other members of it" created circumstances that have disturbed God's intention for your life?

2. What is the legacy of circumstances given you by your immediate family? How have these circumstances enhanced or hindered God's intention for your life?

3. When have you suffered as a result of one of God's natural laws being broken?

4. Think of a time when you reacted positively and creatively to difficult circumstances or great suffering. What good, if any, came of your positive response?

5. Think of another time when you succumbed to suffering or difficulties and let pain or darkness enfold you. What was the eventual outcome?

6. Think of some thorny or baffling problem in your life. Apply the guidelines for cooperating with God's circumstantial will and choose a plan of action:
* my actions will be of use to the community or benefit the common good.
* my actions or attitudes will satisfy a true need or desire (of mine or another).
* my actions are in harmony with my personal and spiritual values.

7. Do you believe in miracles? Does God intervene and change the course of human events? Why or why not?

Exercises

1. Carry a small pad of paper with you one day this week. Whenever you confront a difficult situation jot it down. The situations don't have to be life-changing. For example "car wouldn't start—late for work," "boss takes my idea and tells staff it was hers to begin with," "hassled mother and crying child in front of me in grocery line," "neighbor's son breaks his foot playing soccer and asks me for ride to doctor's office, etc."

At the day's end copy your list on the chart below and reflect on your response to it. In the third column evaluate your response. Give yourself a:

(+) if your actions were of use to the community or benefit the common good
(–) if they were not

(+) if your actions or attitudes satisfied a true need or desire
(–) if they did not

(+) if your actions and attitudes were in harmony with your personal and spiritual values
(–) if they were not

In the final column consider any alternative responses you might have chosen. Ponder how these actions or attitudes might have influenced the circumstances differently.

Difficult Situation	My Response	How Did I Do?	Alternative Response

2. Imagine yourself as a small child after a frustrating day. Find a comfortable, quiet place and envision that you are climbing onto the lap of the one who loves you most. Settle in and tell this one who loves you about your day, your feelings and frustrations. Write down the conversation you'd like to have, or better still say it aloud, then take a few minutes to sit quietly in the warm embrace of love. Likewise, the love of God is present, rest in it awhile.

Worship Resources

Reading for Reflection

We can let ourselves off that desperate question, "Am I in the right place?" "Have I done the right thing?" Of course, we must sometimes acknowledge sins and mistakes and we must try to learn from them; but we should not foster the kind of worry that leads to despair. God's providence means that *wherever* we have got to, *whatever* we have done, that is precisely where the road to heaven begins. However many cues we have missed, however many wrong turnings we have taken, however unnecessarily we may have complicated our journey, the road still beckons, and the Lord still "waits to be gracious" to us. (Isaiah 30:18)

Prayer by Simon Tugwell

Litany[5]

Jesus was the victim of circumstances beyond his control.
Therefore, he can understand us when we are forced to risk long odds.

Yet his helplessness before people never altered his trust in the Lord.
Therefore, he can deliver us when we are tempted to abandon the struggle.

In our hour of trial, when we are beset by an enemy,
Help us to remember you, O Lord in your hour of trial.

When we are betrayed for personal gain,
Help us to remember you, O Lord.

When we are left to face a crisis alone,
Help us to remember you, O Lord.

When we see a stranger where we had expected a friend,
Help us to remember you, O Lord in your hour of trial.

In our hour of trial, when others have done to us their worst,
Help us to remember you, O Lord, in the hour of your trial, and how that nothing in life or death was able to separate you from the love of God.

Benediction

O Lord, when we are sad, tired, lonely and full of suffering, help us to seek refuge in the sanctuary of the soul where we can find our friend, Jesus, who will comfort, support and guide us onward. Amen.

---

5. Everett Tilson and Phyllis Cole, *Litanies and Other Prayers: For the Common Lectionary: Year B* (Nashville: Abingdon, 1990), 77.

CHAPTER
THREE

GOD'S ULTIMATE WILL

There is a sentence at the end of the book of Job which summarizes the message of this section: "I know that thou canst do all things, and that no purpose of thine can be restrained"—or, as Moffatt translates it, "Nothing is too hard for thee."

We have spoken of the intentional will of God—that is, God's original plan for the well-being of his children, an intention spoiled by man's folly and sin. We have spoken of God's circumstantial will, his will within the circumstances set up by man's evil. I want to write here of God's ultimate will, the goal which I believe he reaches, not only *in spite of* all man may do, but even using man's evil to further his own plan.

Turning to the Cross once more as the supreme example, we see again that—

1. The intentional will of God was not that Jesus should be crucified, but that he should be followed;

2. The circumstantial will of God, God's will in the circumstances which men's evil provided, was that Jesus should accept death, but accept it in such a positive and creative way as to lead to

3. God's ultimate will—namely, the redemption of man, winning man back to God, not in spite of the Cross, but using the Cross, born of man's sin, as an instrument to reach the goal of God's ultimate will.

The picture in my mind is that of children playing beside a tiny stream that runs down a mountainside to join a river in the valley below. Very little children can divert the stream and get great fun out of damming it up with stones and earth. But not one of them ever succeeds in preventing the water from reaching the river at last. (Don't press the illustration and remind me that the Royal Engineers could do so!) In regard to God we are very little children. Though we may divert and hinder his purposes, I don't believe we ever finally defeat them; and, though the illustration doesn't carry us so far, frequently our mistakes and sins are used to make another channel to carry the water of God's plans to the river of his purpose.

The omnipotence of God, you perceive, does not mean that by a sheer exhibition of his superior might God gets his own way. If he did, man's freedom would be an illusion and man's moral development would be made impossible. No "end" which God has in mind can be imposed from without; for his end, the at-one-ment of all souls with him, must come from man's choice of God's way, not the imposition of God's will in irresistible might which leaves no room for choice. Power means ability to achieve purpose. Since the purpose is to win man's volition, any activity of God's which denied or suppressed man's volition, in that it would defeat the purpose, would not be a use of power but a confession of weakness and an acceptance of defeat.

When we say, then, that God is omnipotent, we do not mean that nothing can happen unless it is God's will (= intention). We mean that nothing can happen which can *finally* defeat him.

If man is to have a real freedom, and if the community is to be bound together in such a close unity that the one suffers for the many, even as the one gains through the many—if, in a word, life is to be on the family and not on the individual basis, then obviously ten thousand things can happen that God did not intend, and millions of innocent people will suffer through the sins of others. Of this great truth we need no far-fetched illustration. The horror of war and the suffering of innocent people prove it with terrible convincingness.

What is meant by the omnipotence of God is that he will reach at last his ultimate goal, that nothing of value will be lost in the process, however man may divert and dam up the stream of purpose nearest him, and that God—if he cannot use men as his agents—will, though with great pain to himself and to themselves, use them as his instruments. "I know that thou canst do all things, and that no purpose of thine can be restrained."

Here is an illustration which may help. Many years ago there was no such thing as blotting paper. Ink was dried by dusting the page with a light powder. One day in a paper mill one of the workers made a mistake. Let us for the sake of argument say that he committed a sin. Through gross carelessness and inattention to duty he omitted a certain chemical or material, and the result was that the paper was entirely unfitted for writing material. The owner of the mill was angry. It looked as if the mistake meant the sheer loss of the whole material concerned. But when the paper was brought to him and he tried to write on it, he noticed the way the ink was immediately absorbed, and the idea of blotting paper occurred to him. Let us suppose, for the sake of the argument, that the goal of the mill owner was to make money. Then we see that apparent loss was turned to gain. The ultimate end (to make money) was reached when the intention (to make money from writing paper) was defeated and the circumstance thrown up by evil (the worker's careless inattention) was reacted to in a positive and creative way.

Of course no illustration we can devise covers all the ground. From this you might argue, "Very well then, let us not bother what we do, however stupid and careless and sinful we may be. If God can use evil as well as good, let him get on with it. Nothing we do matters."

But here is the old argument which Paul fought with such strength in his Epistle to the Romans. When men said, "Shall we continue in sin, that grace may abound?" he said, "God forbid. We who died to sin, how shall we any longer live therein?" Once we see what sin is—"the raised hand, the clenched fist, the blow in the face of God," as Joseph Parker called it—how can we practice it? It would be like a medical student smashing his mother's head with an ax and saying, "What of it? I have increased my knowledge of the structure of the brain." Sin is the blackest thing in the universe. It is one thing to say, "This evil has been done. How can I win good from it?" It is another thing to say, "I will deliberately do evil in order to win good from it."

Further, though God may *use* an instrument for the achievement of divine purpose, if that instrument is human, he has to pay for his sins. God *used* the Cross, we said, as the instrument of a divine purpose, but that did not stop our Lord from saying of Judas, "It had been good for that man if he had not been born," and again, "It must needs be that offences come; but woe to that man by whom the offence cometh!"

With this clear in our minds, however, the message comes to me in these days with immense comfort. These are days full of loss and pain, of suffering and sorrow. *But they are not days of waste.* They are the fruit of the whole world's sin. To go back to the blotting paper illustration, here is the work of slackness on the part not of one worker but of millions. We will not go back in thought with sentences that begin, "If only in 1918 we had . . . " That is too painful now. The result of that slackness is not wasted paper, but wasted lives, wasted homes, wasted cities, wasted money, wasted energy. But will it be waste? My answer is a ringing No! for the simple reason that I trust the Owner of this great mill of a world that is grinding out his purposes. He doesn't lose his temper and say of this world, "I'm sick of you. I wish I'd never created you."

Gash the earth with your railway cutting, and nature at once gets busy on the scar and covers it with not only the kind of green grass which grew on the surrounding fields but with tender violets and primroses which would not grow until a cleft in the earth provided shelter from the north wind. With evil intent men crucified the Son of God, and within six weeks other men were preaching about the Cross as the instrument of salvation. They hardly once referred to it as the crime of man. They—with a daring almost alarming—spoke of it as a redemptive act of God.

Now the whole world is crucified. But look what is happening! There is a new social conscience. What's all this talk about an education act, about new health provisions, new housing, new city planning? Why, what has that to do with war? There were slums before the war, and bad education and inadequate health provision. War hasn't made them. I tell you that the Spirit of God is at his glorious task. He is making the wrath of man to serve him and further his ultimate will. He is using the moment when men's hearts are awestruck at the horror their own evil has brought upon them, to rouse them to what has always been God's will, so that, awakened and responding, they may, through doing God's circumstantial will, reach his ultimate will as certainly as it would have been reached if his intentional will had been done. For surely the extreme horror of war was not necessary before men could understand God's intention for his children who live in great cities.

A young woman, widowed in an accident, says to me, "Yes, I can see your point in regard to world affairs and civic facilities, but come down to the individual. My man has been killed, and my two little children are left fatherless, and I'm young, and life stretches on in an infinite loneliness. How can God ever reach in my life his ultimate will? His intentional will was surely home and married happiness. His will is defeated forever."

If I offered you a glib answer to that, I should hate myself and you would despise me. I set down the question because I want to be honest and not evade it. And here no one can answer save in faith, for no one can see the end from the beginning. Let me tenderly say one or two things. On Good Friday night eleven men, in the deepest gloom felt like you. They said in their hearts: "We trusted him, we followed him. It was his will to establish his kingdom. He told us so. And evil has been allowed to take him from us. It's the end of everything."

But they were wrong, weren't they? It was only the end of their mistake and the beginning of the most wonderful use of evil which God has ever effected. And if you give way to despair, you are wrong too! And one day, like them, you'll find out how wrong you are *and be sadder at your despair than at your loss.*

For you know your loved one is not lost. He is alive. He is working out a plan. And God is still using him in his plan. Maybe from the other side he's helping you. Can you take up life bravely in spiritual communion with the one you've lost? Can you be father and mother to your little ones? Can you comfort weaker hearts than your own in this dark night of the world? Can you say to yourself with Tennyson

> That nothing walks with aimless feet;
> That not one life shall be destroy'd,
> Or cast as rubbish to the void,
> When God hath made the pile complete?

If so, I'm certain you won't be defrauded, that all will be woven into the pattern, that when you get to the end of the road you will not feel any sense of injustice or any sense of loss. God's intentional will was the fulfillment of your personality via what we might call the mountain stream of years of married life. That stream is now blocked. Are you certain, standing where you stand, with your limited human vision, that God cannot fulfill your personality by any other route? Big words these, but underneath them is the conviction of all the saints and the supreme evidence of the Crucified that God is a Father, that the ultimate meaning of the whole universe is Love, and that God will never fail with one of his family unless that one opposes him forever.

Evil can do terrible things to us. The more I read and think, the more I believe in a Devil. "God lets the Devil have a long rope these days," said a friend of mine, a doctor of divinity, to his mother. "Yes," said the old lady, "but he keeps hold of the end of it himself." God still reigns—a God who is like Jesus, who died to make a dream come true that is better than our wildest dreams. Rest in this thought about God's ultimate will. "Eye hath not seen, nor ear heard, neither have entered into the heart of man, the things which God hath prepared for them that love him." Trust God. Rest in the nature of God. He who began this strange adventure we call human life will also control the end. "I am Alpha and *Omega,* the beginning and the *end,* the first and the *last."* The last word is with God—

> That God, which ever lives and loves,
> One God, one law, one element,
> And one far-off divine event,
> To which the whole creation moves—

"one far-off divine event" whose nature no man may dream, but which we may call the accomplishment of the ultimate will of God.

CHAPTER THREE
WORKBOOK

GOD'S ULTIMATE WILL—God's final realization of divine purposes.

Purpose of the Lesson

To understand that God's ultimate will for my life and the world will be reached. It was God who began this strange adventure we call life and it will be God who will control the end. God can transform evil and redeem sin into stepping-stones that lead to ultimate good.

A Prayer Before You Begin

Loving God, use all of my life circumstances—the good, the evil; my strengths, my weaknesses, my faith and my sins alike—to further your good purposes in the world today.

Key Scripture

"Then [Joseph's] brothers also wept, fell down before him, and said, 'We are here as your slaves.' But Joseph said to them, 'Do not be afraid! Am I in the place of God? Even though you intended to do harm to me, God intended it for good, in order to preserve a numerous people, as he is doing today. So have no fear; I myself will provide for you and your little ones.' In this way he reassured them, speaking kindly to them" (Genesis 50:18-21).

Scripture Background

In Genesis 37-45 the story is told of Joseph, favored son of Jacob, who is sold by his jealous brothers to slave traders. Joseph is sold again to Potiphar, captain of Pharaoh's guard. Joseph distinguishes himself as a responsible servant. Joseph is wrongly accused and imprisoned for trying to assault his master's wife while in prison. Joseph interprets the dreams of some fellow prisoners. After one of the prisoners returns to work for the Pharaoh he remembers Joseph when the Pharaoh has some unexplainable dreams. Joseph is called upon to interpret them. Joseph is made a chief officer over the land. When famine comes Joseph is able to save his family from starvation. Joseph comes to see that being sold into slavery has allowed him to preserve a remnant of his people and thus further God's purposes despite the evil done to him by his brothers.

Key Concepts

- God's ultimate will is the goal which God reaches, not only in spite of all we may do, but even through redeeming evil to further the divine plan.

- Considering the ultimate will of God brings up two important truths about God. The first is God's omnipotence: that God's limitless power can achieve every divine purpose for the world. The second truth is that God may choose to limit this power in order to give human beings the freedom to choose to follow God's ways. This freedom is known as *free will*, the ability of a person to make moral choices or express desires and opinions. Free will gives us freedom of choice and also lays the responsibility for our choices directly on our own shoulders.

- In the New Testament the one who is truly free knows that freedom is given so that we can choose to live in service of God and neighbor. For the Christian, the church is the community of those who freely choose to serve and love God together.

Read the following case study and consider the questions that follow.

CASE STUDY #1   **Peter's Story**

Peter, a nine-month-old with AIDS, joins the household of Renee—a single foster mom—and a foster brother. These three become a family with a large extended community of caregivers. Social workers, church friends, home care workers, and friends are in and out of their home daily. Every day seems precious since Renee is keenly aware that they may not have many years together. Renee, who two years ago decided she wanted children, now has two sons. Two young boys who needed a loving parent now have a committed mom, each other, and a host of friends.

Considerations

1. Rehearse God's intentional will for Peter as you determined it during Lesson One. Now consider if and how God's ultimate will has been accomplished in Peter's life. How can God's ultimate will be done after a tragedy like being infected with a horrible disease?

2. What if Renee had determined that she couldn't cope with two needy children of similar ages? Would God's ultimate will have been thwarted? If someone disobeys God's intention, does God have an alternative plan? What do you think and why?

3. Does everything have to work out perfectly for God's ultimate will to be accomplished?

4. Weatherhead writes, "If man is to have real freedom, and if the community is to be bound together in such a close unity that the one suffers for the many, even as the one gains through the many—if, in a word, life is to be on the family and not on the individual basis, then obviously ten thousand things can happen that God did not intend. . . ." Since we suffer and gain due to the acts of others, how does Peter "suffer" or "gain" through what he has experienced?

For further inquiry, look up these scripture verses:

Genesis 17:1; Exodus 6:2-9; Revelation 4:8 (God's might)

Mark 3:31-35 (Jesus defines the spiritual nature of family)

Psalm 68:5-6 (In God's circumstantial will an extended family is provided to care for orphans, the sick, and the lonely)

Read the following case study and consider the questions that follow.

CASE STUDY #2   **Trina's Story**

After a lengthy separation and several attempts at reconciliation, Ed and Trina divorce. Both complete medical school. Ed joins a general medical practice in his hometown. Trina takes a job in another state as an emergency room physician working with trauma victims, which she loves. Both continue to go to their respective churches, although both feel as outsiders in the church due to their status as divorced people.

Considerations

1. Recall God's intentional will for Trina and Ed as you determined it during Lesson One. Now consider if and how God's ultimate will has been accomplished in Trina's and Ed's lives? How can God's ultimate will be done after a tragedy like divorce?

2. What if Trina or Ed had dropped out of medical school or if they had decided to stay together even though the abuse did not end? Would God's ultimate will have been thwarted? If someone disobeys God's intention, does God have an alternative plan? What do you think and why?

3. Does everything have to work out perfectly for God's ultimate will to be accomplished?

4. Weatherhead writes, "If man is to have real freedom, and if the community is to be bound together in such a close unity that the one suffers for the many, even as the one gains through the many—if, in a word, life is to be on the family and not on the individual basis, then obviously ten thousand things can happen that God did not intend . . . ." Since we suffer and gain due to the acts of others, how do Ed and Trina "suffer" or "gain" through what they have experienced?

For further inquiry, look up these scripture verses:

Mark 10:2-12; Matthew 19:4-9 (Jesus' teaching on marriage and divorce)
1 Corinthians 7:10-16 (God's calling regarding marriage and divorce)
Ephesians 5:21-33 (Mutual submission in marriage)
Ezekiel 16:59-63 (God's everlasting covenant)
Isaiah 54:5-8 (God's compassion)
Isaiah 43:1-2 (God's presence in times of great trial)

Read the following case study and consider the questions that follow.

STUDY #3   **Trinity Church**

Trinity Church continues to worship together on Sunday mornings, to run its low cost day care, and to rent some of its classrooms as office space to community groups and other nonprofit groups during the weekdays. They also rent the sanctuary on Sunday afternoons to a new church for non-English speaking Asian immigrants. A shelter for homeless people occupies the parish hall one weekend a month. The congregation remains small but highly active in the community.

Considerations

1. Recall God's intentional will for Trinity Church as you determined it during Lesson One. Now consider if and how God's ultimate will has been accomplished in the congregation and local community.

2. What if Trinity Church had moved to the suburbs? Would God's ultimate will have been thwarted? If a group of people disobeys or disagrees on God's intention, does God have an alternative plan? What do you think and why?

3. Does everything have to work out perfectly for God's ultimate will to be accomplished?

4. Weatherhead writes, "If man is to have real freedom, and if the community is to be bound together in such a close unity that the one suffers for the many, even as the one gains through the many—if, in a word, life is to be on the family and not on the individual basis, then obviously ten thousand things can happen that God did not intend . . . ." Since we suffer and gain due to the acts of others, how does this congregation "suffer" or "gain" through what they have experienced?

For further inquiry, look up these scripture verses:

John 6:35-40 (the ultimate will of God)
Acts 2:42-47 (early church practices)
1 Peter 2:9-11 (the calling of God's people)

Questions for Personal Reflection

1. Today's lesson focuses on God's ultimate will: the goal which God reaches, not only in spite of all we may do, but even using our evil to further the divine plan. Think of several stories from the Bible (Joseph, David, Ruth and Naomi, etc.). How did the people involved help or hinder God's purposes? Does God's ultimate will prevail?

2. When considering God's ultimate will, we must ask about God's power or omnipotence. In theological terms we are talking about *omnipotence:* the characteristic of God that means God has all power and can achieve the divine purposes for the world.

   Weatherhead says: "Power means ability to achieve purpose." Write your own definition of the word *power*.

3. What then is free will? How much power do we have? There is much debate over how much freedom we have. In simplified terms, Calvinists believe that God elects some to be saved and some to be damned—God casts the deciding ballot. Wesleyans believe that God votes for you, Satan votes against you, and you cast the deciding ballot. What do you believe?

4. If God will win no matter what we do, then why not just do as we please? (Read Romans 6:1-14 for help.)

5. How do the church and its members live freely? (Read Galatians 5:13-15 to understand the relationship between freedom and service.)

Exercises

1. Draw a stream running down a mountainside. Now add boulders, logs, and debris to represent the ways your wrong choices, circumstances or mistakes have temporarily hindered God's purposes. Finally trace an alternate route for the stream to continue downstream. Likewise, let this picture remind you that God's ultimate will is being accomplished in your life.

2. On the chart below read the left-hand column, which details the particular events of Joseph's life. Then do the same with the particular events of your life on the right.

Joseph's Life	**My Life**

1. Early signs of giftedness
    powerful dreams
    leadership urges
	1. Early signs of giftedness

2. Family legacy (good and ill)
    father's favoritism
    brothers' resentment
    father's great faith
	2. Family legacy (good and ill)

3. Betrayal or suffering
    thrown into well
    taken to Egypt as a slave
    false accusations
	3. Betrayal and suffering

4. Acts of grace
    wisdom recognized
    position granted
    made leader over Egypt
    fellow prisoner remembers
        him when Pharaoh has a dream
	4. Acts of grace

5. Free choices
    makes choice to serve well
    decides to forgive brothers
	5. Free choices

6. Ultimate result
    saves family from famine
    family is reconciled
	6. Ultimate result

Worship Resources

Reading for Reflection

Do you believe that everything is a part of a plan, a design, an intervention of God in our affairs? I do. And I am convinced that God's love can transform the darkness of a disaster or the irrationality of an earthquake into an event that can influence, or even completely change, our lives. . . . I came upon this passage in Augustine: "God can permit evil only in so far as he is capable of transforming it into a good."

I Sought and I Found by Carlo Carretto

Litany

Our Father which art in heaven
We acknowledge your omnipotence.

Hallowed be thy name
We worship your goodness.

Thy kingdom come
We follow your way.

Thy will be done
We chose your will.

On earth as it is in heaven.
**We are your people,
now and forevermore.**

Amen.

Benediction

Go with us, Almighty God. Aid us as we trust in you and rest in the assurance that ultimately your will shall be done on earth as it is in heaven. Amen.

CHAPTER
FOUR

DISCERNING
THE WILL OF GOD

Having made the foregoing distinctions in regard to the will of God, we may inquire now whether it can be discerned by us and how. My mental picture for you is that of a man lost in a wood. We need not decide whether it is his own fault that he is lost, or whether he has been misdirected, or whether he has been the victim of some accident. He is asking a question which has often been on people's lips lately: "Where do I go from here?" He feels that there must be a path which is the path of God's will for him in those circumstances, but how can he be sure it is God's way, and how can he be certain that he won't make a mistake?

Let me answer the last question first. To be quite honest he cannot be *certain* until he gets to the end that he won't make a mistake, for he must travel by faith more than by sight. But if he is willing to read the signposts and follow them, he will come out to the place where God wants him to be; and, fortunately, God deals with us where we are. There is an amusing story of a motorist who leaned out of his car and asked a yokel the way to York. The yokel replied, "Well, sir, if I were going to York, I shouldn't start from here." Fortunately God can start with us where we are, and he has ways of showing us the path of his will.

I am quite sure that the greatest help available in discerning the will of God is reached when we deepen our friendship with him. Those who know God are the quickest and surest at discerning his will. Sometimes you will hear men and women in conference discussing a gift which they wish to make to an absent member. Then perhaps someone will say, "Well, I have known him for fifty years. I know what he would like us to do"; and I think, generally speaking, the authority is recognized. Sometimes in interpreting a dead man's will we hear someone say, "I know what he would have liked best"; and knowledge and friendship and love become a qualification for deciding what would be the wishes of the person concerned.

Surely it was the friendship Jesus had with God—if we may call it by so simple a word—that made him so utterly certain at every twist and turn of the tortuous road he trod as to which direction was the will of God. He *almost* lost his way in the Garden; the night was very dark. It was hard to find the way; but, kneeling there in agony of mind, with his magic key—"Nevertheless not what I will, but what thou wilt"—he opened the door that led to death, believing that in those circumstances he must take the path of the Cross.

But, friendship apart, there are numerous signposts which give us some direction, and I would like to speak of them briefly.

1. Conscience may be of lowly origin. Some people think it is a kind of group wisdom gathered through the ages as men found out that some ways of living led to a precipice, and some to a dead end, and some were truly thoroughfares. I know that much scorn can be poured on this lowly voice within our hearts. Men have done evil believing that they followed the dictates of conscience. The voice is distorted by the spiritual level the race has reached and depends on the sensibility of the one who responds to it. Even men of the same generation differ here. One can do things without a qualm of conscience, while another, doing the same thing, would bring himself into a torment of remorse, and it may not necessarily be that either is justified by the facts. For years slavery was uncondemned by the consciences of men, and centuries ahead it will be incredible that our consciences could sleep about slums and war. But when all this has been said, we all recognize a voice that says, "This is right; that is wrong," and that the path of God's will is the former.

2. Then there is the lowly signpost we call "common sense." "I prayed for advice," said a man once, "but nothing happened, and I got no answer to my prayers; so I used my common sense." But who gave him his common sense, and why was it given? If God has placed the machinery for making a judgment within the mind of man, why should he not use it, and why should man regard some uncanny way of receiving direction as more likely to be divine because it is unusual? Surely insight based on a thoughtful appreciation of the situation is more reliable than impulse. At the same time a warning must be uttered, in that sometimes the direction of the will of God is the opposite of that which common sense would dictate. The will of God is sometimes what the world would call "madness."

3. Let us not disregard the value of the advice of a friend. I do not mean the counsel of a professional minister or consultant, but talking over one's difficulties with a wise friend who, because he can see the matter from a different angle, can view the pros and cons dispassionately and, because he is outside the emotional setting of the problem, can often give us the most helpful advice. Of course there are some problems where God's best way of helping us is through the advice of the expert. In a difficult medical or psychological situation we may not have enough knowledge to obtain the maximum wisdom without the expert who has made the field of our particular difficulty his own special study. But here again let us think of the adviser as an instrument God can use, just as he can use our own judgment. Remember two quotations from Browning:

> Hush, I pray you!
> What if this friend happen to be—God?

and again:

God teaches us to help each other so,
Lending our minds out.

Get a friend with Christian insight to lend you his mind in your problem, and God will direct you. I don't mean to imply a necessary identification of what the friend advises with what God wills, but a new angle on your problem will help you to see the latter more clearly.

4. There is another way of using the minds and wisdom of others. We reach it as we read great literature, especially biography and history. Again and again it has been to me of inexpressible comfort to read the biographies of great men. Very few problems there are in our lives which great men and women have not had to face before us; and when we read the Bible, which is a library of every kind of literature, but literature all written from a unique point of view—that of the will and purposes of God—then perhaps most clearly of all are we allowed to share in the guidance which God gives his children as they seek to discern his will.

5. Not enough is made, I feel, of the voice of the Church. Jesus once strongly recommended to people to consult the Church. (Matt. 18:17.) I feel that it is not too strong a thing to say that no church is functioning as it ought to do unless there are fellowship groups in it to which the puzzled member may bring his own problem. He may, indeed, disguise it, saying, "I know a man who . . . ," when the man is himself. But I can say from experience at the City Temple that sometimes direction to a troubled soul who seeks to discern the will of God has come with crystal clearness when a group of detached, thoughtful, loving Christian people has been asked what the mind of God is, and what the will of God is, in a certain situation laid before it.

6. Our Quaker friends make much of what they call "Inner Light," and I entirely support the claims they make. They say that God can speak directly to the human soul and show his will to those who seek him. This is undoubtedly true. I would utter only one word of caution. To follow the practice of the Oxford Groups, to endeavor to blank the mind and then take whatever comes into that mind as the will of God, is fraught with a great danger. We are liable to fall into the fallacy of supposing that the method by which we receive this "light" makes it divine, but the thought or impulse that comes to the blank mind is just as much the fruit of earlier mental processes as is, for instance, the thought that comes to the mind after a long argument. Actually one cannot blank the mind or disengage it at any point from all that has gone before. It is as impossible as isolating a wave of the sea and supposing that it has no relation to the waves behind it and the waves before it. Yet if the method is used with wisdom and caution, and if what "comes" in the quiet time is tested by some other ways indicated above or, as the Groupers say, "checked up" with others, no one who knows the facts would deny that God's will is often discerned in this way.

In these ways, then, the will of God, at the point at which we need help, may be discerned. Let me underline that last phrase—*at the point at which we need help*. Sometimes I have made a mistake myself by trying to discern the will of God for years ahead. I have come to the conclusion that God does not encourage us to see too far ahead. One simply must accept the fact that one has no idea where the road one is treading is going to lead. Suffice it to say that when one gets to the crossroads one will know which way to turn, and although we like to think that it is terribly important not to make a mistake—and I repeat one can never be certain that one has not made a mistake—yet I adhere earnestly to the view expressed in the section on the ultimate will of God. Our mistakes, if made in good faith, will not result in our being lost. "We shall not miss our providential way." God often wonderfully weaves mistakes into his plan, as he also weaves our sufferings and our sins.

Let me end this section, however, with two challenging questions which I put to myself and would pass on to you.

1. Do I really want to discern God's will, or do I want to get his sanction for my own? An amusing story is told of a minister who was invited to a church at which the salary was four times what he was already receiving; and, being a devout man, he spent many hours in prayer seeking to discern the will of God. One day a friend met the minister's little boy in the street and said, "Well, what is your father going to do?"

"Well," said the little boy, "Father's praying, but Mother's packing."

The father was saying to God, "What wilt thou have me to do?" and the mother, no less good-intentioned, was saying to God, "This is what I am going to do. I hope you will approve."

Discerning the will of God does really mean putting ourselves out of the picture—not choosing a way as his because it is unpleasant (we have dealt already with that fallacy), but certainly not going to the other extreme and saying, "This is what I am going to do. Please approve, because I want so badly to do it."

2. The second challenging question is this: Have I got the courage to do God's will when I discern it? Many people ask a great many questions as to how they may find the will of God, and every minister knows what it is to sit down with an inquiring person in order to find out the answer to the question. But most ministers have also had experience of those people who, seeing clearly the will of God, say, "No, anything but that." It is only because I see this weakness in myself that I would pass on to others the warning that usually what one needs is not discernment but grit. For myself, more than I need discernment I need fortitude, courage, faith, determination, and perseverance. Not to see, merely, but to do. As Drinkwater puts it:

> Knowledge we ask not—knowledge Thou hast lent,
> But, Lord, the will—there lies our bitter need,
> Give us to build above the deep intent
>   The deed, the deed.

CHAPTER FOUR
WORKBOOK

DISCERNING THE WILL OF GOD—The Ways God Guides Us.

Purpose of the Lesson

To discover ways we can discern God's will by deepening our friendship with God.

A Prayer Before You Begin

O God, I give this time to you. If there is anything I need to hear and heed, speak to me and guide me that I may know your will in all the matters of my life.

Key Scriptures

"Trust in the LORD with all you heart, and do not rely on your own insight. In all your ways acknowledge him, and he will make straight your paths" (Proverbs 3:5-6).

Scripture Background

The Proverbs in the Bible are a collection of poems and sayings meant to instruct the young on how to cope with life through reverencing God, paying attention, practicing self-control and cultivating wisdom. The key scriptures for this lesson remind us that trusting in the Lord is a wholehearted endeavor, not something we do just in times of trouble or confusion. Acknowledging God demands more than simple lip service to God's existence; it requires personal awareness of and obedience to God's ways.

Key Concepts

- God can start with us where we are, and God has a way of showing us the path of his will. The greatest help available in discerning the will of God is reached when we deepen our friendship with God. Those who know God are the quickest and surest at discerning God's will.

- The way to discern God's will is to cultivate a relationship with God. The "tools" or "methods" we use may vary, but all people of faith practice some type of spiritual discipline in order to set aside time regularly to meet with, pray to, and honor God.

- Six of the "numerous signposts that give us some direction" are:

1. Conscience: Listening to the lowly voice within our hearts that says, "This is right; that is wrong," and that the path of God's will is the former.

2. Common Sense: Using our God-given ability to make judgments. An insight based on a thoughtful assessment of the situation is more reliable than impulse. Yet, be forewarned that sometimes the will of God is the opposite of that which common sense would dictate. The will of God is sometimes what the world would call "madness."

3. Advice of friend: Asking a wise friend who can give sound advice since he or she sits outside of the emotional setting of the problem.

4. Reading the Bible and great literature, especially biography and history: Few if any problems we face have not been faced earlier by great men and women before us. Through seeking to see God's action in their lives, we may discern help for our own.

5. Voice of the Church: Bring the problem to a group of thoughtful, loving people outside of the situation and seek the will of God. A Quaker clearness meeting provides an example. This type of meeting is initiated to seek guidance for some individual's question be it for vocational clarity, premarital guidance, or even business decisions.[6]

6. Inner Light: Listen for God to speak directly through silence and prayer. What comes to mind as God's spoken word should be validated through one of the other signposts, as it is sometimes difficult to distinguish from our own desires and God's will.

---

6. For further description of this type of guidance see "The Discipline of Guidance" in *Celebration of Discipline* by Richard J. Foster (San Francisco: HarperCollins, 1978), 150-62.

Read the following case study and consider the questions that follow.

CASE STUDY #1   **Peter's Story**

Peter soon is a full part of the family. He and his brother squabble over toys and ask for each other first thing in the morning. However, life remains very difficult. Renee repeatedly must decide life-and-death issues, like whether to allow Peter to be enrolled in an experimental drug trial. After one particularly difficult hospitalization, Renee agonizes long and hard before determining to place Peter in the study, as the preliminary results point toward enhancing the immune system's ability to fight off one of the painful opportunistic diseases Peter has suffered from several times. She bases her decision on hours of conversation with committed friends, prayer, and a conviction that it is worth taking a risk to enhance Peter's immune system to ward off recurrent bouts of painful illness and thus upgrade his quality of life.

Still, at moments she wonders if she has discerned God's will.

Considerations

1. Put yourself in Renee's position. You are the parent of a child with a life-threatening disease. To whom would you go for advice? How would you reach such a decision?

2. Once a decision has been made, what would you do to follow through with the decision in a faithful and ethical manner?

3. What do you do if a close friend or family member opposes your decision?

4. Weatherhead says, "God does not encourage us to see too far ahead. One simply must accept the fact that one has no idea where the road one is treading is going to lead." Is Renee making decisions too far in advance? Should she wait? Why is it helpful to think through difficult decisions before the moment of crisis, tragedy, or death?

For further inquiry, look up these scripture verses:

Psalm 42 (deep calls to deep)
Psalm 63:1-8 (seeking God)

Read the following case study and consider the questions that follow.

CASE STUDY #2   The Story of Ed and Trina

Ed settled into his hometown practice and remarried. His new wife did not feel called to missions, thus Ed never applied for missionary service. Trina went on several short-term mission trips and as a result was offered a two-year position overseeing a pediatric clinic in a developing nation. She is torn, as she loves working as an emergency room physician. Most of her friends encourage her to go overseas, as this has been a long-term dream. Her church promises financial support. Trina reads all she can of early medical missionaries and is especially moved by the late-eighteenth-century story of Ida Scudder, the daughter of medical missionaries who did not want to be a missionary like her parents. One night Ida was asked by a Brahmin, another Hindu, and a Muslim to help deliver babies in difficult childbirth situations. They refused help from her father, as custom prohibited close contact between women and unrelated men. Early the next morning she heard the village drums heralding the news of death. Each of the women she had assisted died during the night. Ida then felt called to prepare for medical missions to help the women of India. Ida spent more that fifty years in medical missions in India and established a modern medical complex in Vellore.[7]

After reading Ida's story, Trina dreams about three people coming to beg for her help—a homeless man, a battered wife, and a child injured in a car accident. All three had been emergency room patients for whom Trina had cared. Trina decides to remain at home in her present job. She now believes that her mission field is right in the community where she lives.

She wonders if she has discerned God's will.

Considerations

1. Put yourself in Trina's position. You are offered an opportunity to fulfill a lifelong dream. Who would you go to for advice? How would you reach such a decision?

---

7. For more on Ida Scudder, see Ruth A. Tucker, *From Jerusalem to Irian Jaya: A Biographical History of Christian Missions* (Grand Rapids: Zondervan, 1983), 332-36.

2. Once a decision has been made, what would you do to follow through with the decision in a faithful and ethical manner?

3. What would you do if a close friend or family member opposes your decision?

4. Weatherhead says, "God does not encourage us to see too far ahead. One simply must accept the fact that one has no idea where the road one is treading is going to lead." Is Trina making decisions too far in advance? Should she wait? Why is it helpful to think through difficult decisions before the moment of crisis, tragedy or death?

For further inquiry, look up these scripture verses:

Romans 11:29 (irrevocable nature of God's call)
Romans 12:4-8 (use of gifts)
2 Corinthians 5:17-21 (the ministry of reconciliation)

Read the following case study and consider the questions that follow.

CASE STUDY #3   **Trinity Church**

Just before Easter an early morning fire destroys the sanctuary of Trinity Church. Thankfully, no one is hurt, but the many groups that use the building are dismayed. The building is adequately insured, and now church leaders again must decide whether to rebuild or use the money to relocate to another part of the city. When the fire investigators file their report, they conclude that an arsonist started the fire. This leads many to conclude that the church needs to move to a safer neighborhood. They reason, "The church has already dwindled, perhaps the fire is just God's way of giving us the resources to relocate to a place where a larger congregation could be built up." Others counter that the dire needs of the neighborhood are precisely the reasons they should rebuild on the same spot.

The church leaders call the church to prayer and study for a month, to better understand the mission of the church. At month's end they call a community-wide meeting to get the input of neighborhood agencies and groups. Then the church gathers for what the pastor calls a "body-life meeting." At this meeting everyone is invited to share what they learned during the month-long study of the mission of the church. When all who wish to speak have spoken, the minister directs everyone to sit silently together for a lengthy period of silent prayer.

Lastly, a written vote is taken. When the votes are tabulated, a clear majority has voted to rebuild.

A few vocally wonder if they have discerned God's will.

Considerations

1. Put yourself in the position of a member of Trinity Church. What would you do if your church suffered a disaster? To whom would you go to for advice? How would you reach such a decision? Would you participate if your church leaders followed a similar process to the one described above?

2. Once a decision has been made, what would you do to follow through with the decision in a faithful and ethical manner?

3. What would you do if a close friend or family member opposes the decision? What if you were one of the few who voted to relocate?

4. Weatherhead says, "God does not encourage us to see too far ahead. One simply must accept the fact that one has no idea where the road one is treading is going to lead." Did Trinity Church make a hasty decision? Should they have waited? Is it good to determine the mission of the church after a disaster? What if the church is rebuilt and the congregation remains small. Have they done the right thing?

For further inquiry, look up these scripture verses:

Galatians 5:16-25 (walk by the spirit)
1 Thessalonians 5:11-24 (Christian life together)

Questions for Personal Reflection

Before asking for God's specific guidance ask yourself:

1. Do I really want to discern God's will, or do I want to get his sanction for my own?
2. Do I have the courage to do God's will when I discern it?
3. Weatherhead advises that "the will of God, at the point at which we need help, may be discerned." At what point of need do you find yourself?
4. Is what you seek guidance for too far in the future to be discerned? Is God asking you to wait and pay closer attention to other matters that are directly at hand?

Exercises

1. Identify one specific need for which you need God's guidance.

During each day this week seek the wisdom from one of the six signposts or disciplines outlined in this week's study. It would be helpful to reflect on what you discern by writing in a journal or recording your thoughts on a cassette recorder. At week's end you can then examine the guidance received from all six ways of seeking God's will.

Day one: Conscience: Listen to the lowly voice within your heart. Write down the pros and cons of any decision that you are weighing. Ponder each choice. Do you sense your conscience saying "This is right; that is wrong" about any of the choices? Do any of them make you feel uneasy? Do any of them energize you? Pay attention to your responses when considering each choice.

Day two: Common sense: Use your God-given ability to make judgments. An insight based on a thoughtful assessment of the situation is more reliable than impulse. What would common sense have you do?

Day three: The Advice of a friend: Ask a wise friend who can give you sound advice, since he or she sits outside the emotional setting of the problem. If you don't know to whom to talk, pray that God will bring someone to mind. Then contact that person. You need not tell the person every detail of your dilemma. Share only what you are comfortable in sharing.

Day four: Read a Bible story or the biography of a great person of God: Few if any problems have not been faced earlier by great men and women. Through seeking to see God's action in their lives you may discern help for your own.[8]

---

8. There are different ways of reading the Bible. You may wish to study a particular book of the Bible or use a concordance to look up a specific issue and read passages throughout the Bible. You also may want to practice *lectio divina*, the ancient practice of reading a passage of scripture until a phrase or word catches your attention. Then repeat that phrase and meditate upon it letting the wisdom of scripture rain down on you like warm rain. Then ask the Holy Spirit to teach you the lesson that scripture has for you today.

Both ways of reading the Bible are important. Knowing what the Bible says and letting the Bible speak directly to you as a word from God are equally helpful ways of discerning God's will.

If you wish to read great Christian biography or church history to illuminate your discernment process and do not know where to begin, ask your minister, a local Christian bookstore owner, or a well-read member of your church for recommendations.

Day five: Voice of the Church: Share your question with a small Bible-study group or home fellowship, or invite two or three prayerful friends over for coffee. Ask them to be companions as you discern God's will. They should not be asked to make the decision for you or assume that whatever advice they give must be followed. This is a process to aid in clarity, not to give over to others the authority for your decision-making.

Day six: Inner Light: Listen for God to speak directly through silence and prayer. Choose a private, quiet place to pray. Sit upright and attentively. Try to clear your mind of distractions. If you are distracted by something, simply acknowledge the distraction, bring it before God and release it. Refocus your attention and continue for an extended period of time.

What comes to mind as God's word should be validated through one of the other signposts, as it is sometimes difficult to distinguish between our own desires and God's will.

Worship Resources

Reading for Reflection

The spiritual life is not achieved by denying one part of life for the sake of another. The spiritual life is achieved only by listening to all of life and learning to respond to each of its dimensions wholly and with integrity.

Wisdom Distilled from the Daily by Joan Chittister

Group Worship Activity

Take a piece of colored paper and a marker or other writing utensil. Tear the paper into pieces and decorate them to represent the bits of wisdom you received this week in discerning God's will. Arrange the pieces of paper on a tabletop or tape them on another piece of paper to create a multicolored mosaic. Let the mosaic remind you that God's will is discerned from seeking guidance from several sources. If this activity is done with a group, create a collective mosaic. Recall that the cumulative wisdom points us in the direction of God's will.

Benediction

O Lord,
  you know me.
You know when I sit
  and when I stand.
You have me always present
  in your mind.
For this, Lord, I thank you.
You know the path for my life
  and what is best for me.
Lord, reveal to me the path
  I am to walk.
Bless me and guide me
  and be Lord to me
so that whichever road I take
  I may do all for your glory.
In Jesus' name. Amen.

—"Vocation Prayer" from the Beech Grove Benedictine Community[9]

---

9. Used by permission of the Beech Grove Benedictine Community, Beech Grove, Indiana.

CHAPTER
FIVE

"IN HIS WILL IS OUR PEACE"

In this section I should like the reader to have in his mind not only the sentence of Dante which stands at the head, "In his will is our peace," but also a word of God for us in the book of Proverbs: "In all thy ways acknowledge him, and he shall direct thy paths."

We may feel that it was all very well for Dante to say, "In his will is our peace"; but there are so many things happening in the world to-day that are outside his will—at any rate in the sense of being outside his intention—that we may feel debarred from peace. Exactly! That is why we do not find peace, but instead war without and restlessness within. After all the years of war it is not surprising to find so many people ill. If not incapacitated in body, thousands are anxious and worried and sleepless. But on top of it, if a man has any imagination or sensitiveness left, and lets his mind brood over the slaughter and suffering, the worry and unhappiness of this war-stricken world, his mind is continually wounded, and the power of the mind over the body is so great that one almost feels it is true to say that only those can feel well who are living, both mentally and physically, remote from the horror of war, or who somehow, by virtue of their temperament or their indifference or by the skillful practice of looking the other way, have built up a wall of defense between themselves and the bleeding world around them. For most of us there is the dull sorrow which goes on day after day, and which then is suddenly focused into some poignant case of suffering, thrusting itself upon our attention because the sufferer is dear to us, or because he chooses us as the recipient of his burden. One is glad when he finds the relief of a burden shared, but sometimes some of us feel we do not know how to go on for another day. We are so burdened down that we even feel impatient with Dante, and say, "Yes, but all this is not his will, and therefore how may peace be found?"

Here should come, I think, the value of our earlier thinking and our distinction between the intentional, the circumstantial, and the ultimate will of God.

We saw that even though the intentional will of God is deflected by man's misuse of free will—by the folly and ignorance in the world, and by that family relationship through which all humanity is so closely bound together that your sins affect me and my sins hurt you—yet, even so, there is *a* will of God within the circumstances which evil has caused. I believe, as we have said before, that the Cross was not the intention of God for Jesus. God's intention was that Jesus should be followed, not crucified. But when evil men thrust the Cross upon him, he accepted God's will in those circumstances and so reacted to them that he made his Cross an instrument of power by which the ultimate will of God could be done. In the Garden of Gethsemane, when the shadows were falling upon him, he saw, like Bunyan's pilgrim, the bright Light; and by keeping on the path that led to it, he achieved God's purposes not only in spite of the Cross, but through it.

So the message of this section is that no evil circumstances can ever befall us but we can find in them a path which is God's way for us just then, and we must train ourselves, as we saw in the last section, so to discern the will of God that we shall not falter or fail to find the path. When we find it, then, though all the world is in tumult, there is at least an inner peace at the core of our being—a peace that comes from knowing that we are within his will and his will is revealed to us in those circumstances and at that moment.

To be within God's will means peace for three reasons:

1. We lose the fear of getting lost. Everyone knows the terror of the child who cannot find the path that leads to home. There is a good illustration for us here in the way an airman finds his way home. A radio beam is sent out from his own home station, and once in that beam he has only to follow it to find his way. If he goes out of that directing beam a buzzer sounds in his earphones, telling him clearly enough: "You are going wrong. You must get back until all is quiet." In the home beam there is peace. I think it is not stretching the illustration to say that God sends out, as it were, a beam of direction—namely, his will for us in those circumstances in which we find ourselves—and as long as we keep in his will there is peace. It is when we go out of it or cannot find it—and this can be our case sometimes, however hard we try, as I know to my sorrow—that disturbance and unrest are set up in our minds.

I suspect that the same thing happens in the brain of a bird. We must not talk of the "courage" and "trust" of the swallow, for these are values which have no meaning in birdland. But in the spring or early summer a swallow away in Africa will start off on a journey of thousands of miles, and come back to the eaves of the same little village church among the elms where she built her nest last year. She will not be deflected or lose her way. She will find an unknown path through storms and driving winds and across the leagues of sea without disturbance, fretting, or anxiety, because, although mechanically, she is in the path of God's will, and in his will there is peace. So, says Browning:

> I go to prove my soul!
> I see my way as birds their trackless way.
> I shall arrive! what time, what circuit first,
> I ask not. . . .
> In some time, his good time, I shall arrive.

Let us take this message to heart, that by keeping within the will of God, as we see it in any experience, we find our way even though apparently overwhelming storms, until we arrive at last where God wants us to be—and the goal of all human endeavor is to fulfill God's purposes and to be one with him.

2. The second reason why I think we find peace within the will of God is this: The dread of carrying the responsibility of what happens is removed. What a dreadful moment it was when the crowd, intent on the crucifixion of Christ, shouted out: "His blood be on us, and on our children." They were asserting that they were quite ready to take the responsibility for their actions. It is that responsibility which so often weighs us down. But I believe God's message to us includes this: it is as though he said, "As long as you try to do my will, I will accept responsibility for whatever happens. I will carry that burden for you. I will direct you, and the consequences are my responsibility, not yours." "In all thy ways acknowledge him, and he shall direct thy paths."

Perhaps an illustration will serve here. I heard recently of a little girl whose mother was away from home, so that the child had the task of housekeeping for her father and several smaller brothers or sisters. One can only imagine the burden of responsibility which the child carried, as she tried to fill her mother's place, not only in keeping house, but in answering the demands of the smaller children. She bore up bravely and carried through her duties splendidly, but when her mother came back, one can imagine the relief of the little girl as she cried, "Oh, Mummy, I'm so glad you have come." Remember that the child probably still did most of the duties that she had been doing before, but her mother bore the responsibility. I feel that the illustration goes a good way, that when we submit our will to the will of God, in a sense we can say to God, "I'm so glad you have come." We are not any longer carrying out a set of duties in loneliness and bearing the responsibility of life alone. We are trying to do the will of One who is all the time there, and who says to us: "All you have to do is to follow the plan of my will from day to day, and the responsibility for what happens I will carry for you." Instead of that we are trying to bear in the world what is God's burden of responsibility.

I wonder if I might further illustrate by quoting part of a prayer which I wrote down for my own comfort recently, during some very heavy days of strain:

> Lord Jesus, Bearer of men's burdens, Comforter of the sorrowful, we would bring to thee all whose hearts are sad. Help us to mediate thy strengthening sympathy to others, but grant that we may be so continually refreshed by our companionship with thee that we may not be crushed by the world's burdens. Thou art the burden bearer—not we. Thou art the Redeemer—not we. Thou alone, O Christ, canst in thy strong heart carry the woes of the world. In this faith, teach us to do our duty day by day as we see it to be thy will, and save us from the depression of those who try to carry more than man was made to bear, and ever to look to thee, O Lamb of God who bearest the sins of the world.

3. The third reason why God's will means our peace is that in his will our conflicts are resolved. I am aware that an element of conflict is essential to the progress of the soul. The soul that is unconscious of any conflict would be one ceasing to recognize a clash of good and evil—the soul so dulled by acquiescence to impulse that temptation had lost its power, the thing desired being done without conflict. A dreadful deterioration of personality would follow. At the same time, how weak is the man who constantly weighs "Shall I do this?" with

"Shall I do that?" The guiding principle "I will do God's will as far as I can see it" is one that answers a great many of our conflicts and therefore brings us peace and strength. If it be said, "Yes, but you could end conflict by deciding to do wrong," my answer is that doing wrong always sets up a dozen conflicts where formerly there was one. We wade more and more deeply into the morass of evil and are exhausted in the attempts to get out of it, for the trend of the universe is toward goodness.

> For the everlasting right
> The eternal stars are strong.

If this were a psychological lecture, I should try to explain how often the personality is exhausted by these conflicts. As I write these words, I recall a young officer in the A.T.S. who once consulted me, complaining of a fatigue so great that at times she could not lift her arms above shoulder level in order to do her hair. Her mind was tormented by the obsession that she would fall ill. The truth was that part of her mind wanted to fall ill because illness would bring sympathy, love, the security of home, and her parents' care. A recent love affair which had been broken off had deprived her of love, and she craved the love of her mother. But another part of her mind feared illness, since illness in her case, for which there was no real cause, would only be a guilt-causing get-out from the Army life that she hated and in which there was no chance of being loved. The hunger for love and the deprivation of love are known to every psychologist as fruitful causes of neurosis.

Again and again these conflicts weaken and exhaust us. A young girl feels the conflict between duty to her mother and a desire for independence. Dr. Hadfield tells us that in the mind of a soldier the sense of duty was so much in conflict with the desire to run away, promoted by the self-preservation instinct, that a condition of paralysis of the legs was produced which solved the immediate problem but of course disabled the patient. In our own psychological clinic I have known the conflict in a student between the desire to excel, as he had done at school, and the inferiority which he felt so keenly when proceeding to the university, where he found himself among those of finer mental caliber than he had met at school. The frustration of not being, as it were, top of the class any longer, the fear of being found out to be ordinary, and the desire for the top places even in the university produced a conflict so exhausting as to disable the patient altogether. Hadfield wisely says: "By facing our conflicts and deliberately making our choice, by directing all our endeavors to one great purpose, confidently and fearlessly, the soul is restored to harmony and strength."

I always imagine that the lovely picture Jesus painted in his phrase, "Take my yoke upon you, and learn of me; for I am meek and lowly in heart: and ye shall find rest unto your souls," is really that of the strong ox yoked with the weaker, untried animal. The weaker has to pull only his own weight, as we say, and keep level with the stronger. The stronger carries the heavy end of the yoke. The stronger is responsible for the straight furrow and for reaching the end of it. If the weaker keeps pulling out into a direction of his own, the yoke chafes his shoulders, and the burden becomes heavy. "Take my yoke upon you," says Jesus, "and learn of me to be meek and lowly in heart. Don't be self-opinionated and proud and self-assertive, saying, 'I'm going my own way.' By doing that you make the yoke chafe your shoulders. Walk with me, and it becomes easy (in the true sense of that word). The responsibility is taken from you, and the burden becomes light." "In his will is our peace."

In my early teens I often had a holiday at a farmhouse in the Charnwood Forest. Near the farm there was one rocky crag on which I loved to sit, especially at sunset hour. Below my feet the hillside ran steeply down to a big reservoir, fringed with reeds and rushes. Then there was the expanse of water, and on the other side of it a grand red granite crag, rising sheer from the lake and crowned with stately pines. I have sat there in silence at all hours of the day. I can close my eyes now and recover the sense of calm and peace that came to me in that lonely spot. I can almost hear the cry of the coot in the rushes, the lovely whisper of the wind in the bracken, and the chattering of the water among the stones of a tiny beach between the reeds. One day there came to me, almost as a revelation, a thought which may be quite a platitude to you, but which struck my mind with the shock of truth. There was no human being or even human habitation in sight. Everything I could see was fulfilling perfectly the will of God. Agreed that that will was mechanically done and that the wild life around me had no burden of choice, but I seemed to learn the secret of the harmony and peace of that spot. The will of God was perfectly done. If we could do voluntarily that which is done in nature mechanically, I believe we should find the same sense of peace. "In all thy ways acknowledge him [as the birds do], and he shall direct thy paths."

The poets say these things better than we do. Let me conclude with some verses of the poet William Cullen Bryant, written as he watched the figure of a wild bird flying, as it seemed, into the heart of the sunset:

> Whither, 'midst falling dew,
> While glow the heavens with the last steps of day,
> Far, through their rosy depths, dost thou pursue
> Thy solitary way?
>
> Vainly the fowler's eye
> Might mark the distant flight to do thee wrong,
> As, darkly painted on the crimson sky,
> Thy figure floats along.
>
> Seek'st thou the plashy brink
> Of weedy lake, or marge of river wide,
> Or where the rocking billows rise and sink
> On the chafed ocean side?
>
> There is a Power whose care
> Teaches thy way along that pathless coast,—
> The desert and illimitable air,—
> Lone wandering, but not lost.
>
> Thou'rt gone, the abyss of heaven
> Hath swallowed up thy form; yet, on my heart
> Deeply hath sunk the lesson thou hast given,
> And shall not soon depart.
>
> He who, from zone to zone,
> Guides through the boundless sky thy certain flight,
> In the long way that I must tread alone
> Will lead my steps aright.

CHAPTER FIVE
WORKBOOK

"IN HIS WILL IS OUR PEACE"—Finding rest in tumultuous times.

Purpose of the Lesson

To understand that living out God's will as far as we know it will bring us inner peace.

A Prayer Before You Begin

God, help me to do your will as far as I can see it. May I be at peace knowing that I am walking the path that you have set.

Key Scripture

"Now may the God of peace, who brought back from the dead our Lord Jesus, the great shepherd of the sheep, by the blood of the eternal covenant, make you complete in everything good so that you may do his will, working among us that which is pleasing in his sight, through Jesus Christ, to whom be the glory forever and ever. Amen." (Hebrews 13:20-21).

Scripture Background

This passage is the benediction to a letter written to a group of Christians who are afflicted by weariness and may have been facing persecution. In the letter to the Hebrews the author exhorts this group to "hold firm" to their confidence, faith and hope. The Hebrews are to emulate the great forebears of the faith, Abraham and Sarah, Moses, Rahab, David, and "so great a cloud of witnesses" who held fast to faith in the midst of adversity. The Hebrews, and all who read the letter, are exhorted to "run with perseverance the race that is set before us, looking to Jesus the pioneer and perfecter of our faith" (12:1-2). For it is through obedience to God's will that the God of peace makes us "complete in everything good" (13:21).

Key Concepts

- No evil circumstances can ever befall us that we cannot find in them a path that is God's way for us just then, and we must train ourselves to discern the will of God that we shall not falter or fail to find the path. When we find it, then, though all the world is in tumult, there is at least an inner peace at the core of our being—a peace that comes from knowing we are within his will and his will is revealed to us in those circumstances and at that moment.

- When we are within the will of God we can be at peace for three reasons:

  1. We lose the fear of getting lost. Since we are where God wants us to be, we can be confident that we are on the right path, no matter how difficult or confusing the present may be.

  2. The dread of carrying the responsibility of what happens is removed. When we are living within the will of God, the division of responsibility is clear: God is the burden bearer, and we are the obedient followers.

  3. In God's will our conflicts are resolved. When doing God's will becomes our guiding purpose, many of our questions and struggles are harmonized or clarified by our obedience.

Read the following case study and consider the questions following it.

CASE STUDY #1   **Peter's Story**

Renee learns after making the decision to enroll Peter in the pediatric trials for a new drug that he will have to travel to another state a few days each month to be monitored by national experts. While the travel will be taxing on Peter—and on Renee, as she must accompany him—she wrestles with questions about her other son. What will the absence do to him? Who will care for him? Still, she trusts her decision and feels that a provision will become clear in time. She tells everyone she knows about her dilemma, and soon a local health agency offers money to provide transportation for Peter's brother so that they can be together during the treatment times.

For Renee this provision confirms that the decision has been made within the will of God, because things are working out for the good of her entire family.

Considerations

1. What were Renee's guiding principles for acting on her previous decision? What gave her confidence to move ahead even when the details weren't clear?

2. In this situation, what is Renee's responsibility and what is God's?

3. What brought Renee peace of mind? Imagine you were in similar circumstances. What would assure you?

For further inquiry, look up these scripture verses:

Psalm 85:8 (the promise of peace)
Isaiah 26:3 (perfect peace)
John 14:25-27 (the peace of Christ)

Read the following case study and consider the questions that follow.

CASE STUDY #2   Trina's Story

Many people are dismayed by Trina's decision to stay at her job in the emergency ward of a local hospital instead of accepting a position in a mission hospital overseas. When state budget cuts make her job more difficult, she wonders whether she made the right decision, but during moments of prayerful reflection she remains confident that she is where she is supposed to be.

A local homeless shelter hears about Trina's commitment to the underserved in the community and asks her to advise their staff nurse on how to develop an outreach program for pregnant women and mothers of small children who are homeless. Trina is thrilled. She feels God is honoring her decision to follow what she discerned to be God's will for her life.

Considerations

1. What were Trina's guiding principles for acting on her previous decision? What gave her confidence to move ahead even when the details weren't clear?

2. In this situation, what is Trina's responsibility and what is God's?

3. What brought Trina peace of mind? Imagine you were in similar circumstances. What would assure you?

For further inquiry, look up these scripture verses:

Matthew 25:31-45 (caring for the least of these)

Matthew 28:18-20 (Jesus' commission to the disciples)

Read the following case study and consider the questions that follow.

CASE STUDY #3   **Trinity Church**

Rebuilding Trinity Church proves to be very difficult. Construction delays, cost overruns, and resistance from a few neighbors distressed over noise and heavy equipment in the area provide one headache after another for the church leadership. After one particularly difficult series of events, one church member reminds the church of the strong sense of rightness they felt when they voted to rebuild. He then declares his intent to move closer to the church to be of assistance in the process and challenges others to do likewise.

He and his family rent an apartment across the street from the church and begin to keep in daily contact with the builders. They also get to know the neighbors and cultivate relationships with those who oppose the church rebuilding. They invite all who are interested to a weekly potluck and Bible study in their apartment. When the final permits come up before the city council the neighborhood representatives voice no further objections.

The membership of Trinity Church is full of praise and relief. They feel certain that they are following God's will for their church.

Considerations

1. What were the church leaders' guiding principles for acting on their previous decision? What gave them confidence to move ahead even when the details weren't clear?

2. In this situation, what is Trinity Church's responsibility and what is God's?

3. What brought the church members peace of mind? Imagine you were in similar circumstances. What would assure you?

For further inquiry, look up these scripture verses:

Ephesians 2:14-22 (Jesus is our peace)
Philippians 4:6-7 (the peace of God)
Colossians 3:12-17 (let the peace of Christ rule in your hearts)

Questions for Personal Reflection

1. What inner turmoil or worry is currently distracting you from experiencing God's peace?

2. Have you ever experienced the assurance of inner peace? Describe that feeling and time. Was everything in your life easy? If not, why do you think you felt at peace even though times were difficult?

3. What community or world events especially tear at your heart and cause distress? Why do you think you feel concern or compassion for these dire needs?

4. For Jesus, the cross that was an instrument of mortal suffering became an instrument of power by which the ultimate will of God could be done. What is your cross—the agent of pain or suffering in your life? Can it become an instrument of transformation? Why or why not?

5. Are you carrying a responsibility or burden that is rightly God's to shoulder? Can you lay it down? What specific act of laying down a burden not meant for you to carry will you do today?

6. The guiding principle to answer a great many of our conflicts is "I will do God's will as far as I can see it." What specifically do you know of God's will for you? Write it down.

Exercises

1. Below is a yoke—a wooden frame that joins two burden bearers so that they can work together. There is an old legend that says that Jesus, the carpenter, made the best ox yoke in Galilee. Over his carpenter shop hung the sign "My yokes fit well." What burdens must God shoulder for you? List them in the indicated spaces.

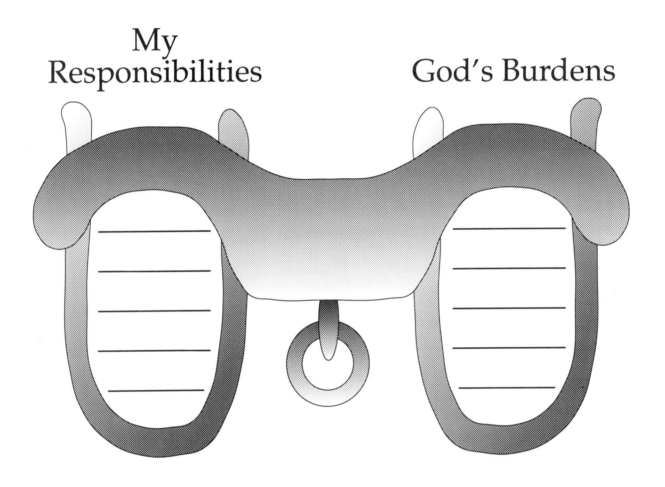

My
Responsibilities

God's Burdens

2. Look at a world map and identify the areas of extraordinary suffering. Prayerfully place the peace of these areas into God's hands and listen to hear whether God has a job for you in helping to alleviate this suffering.

3. Reread Weatherhead's description of Charnwood Forest on page 79. What place in your experience conjures this same sense of calm and rest? Find a picture or reminder of that place and secure it on your desk or in your workplace to remind you of what the will of God perfectly done looks and feels like.

Worship Resources

Reading for Reflection

After we have made a decision in accordance with God's will, we receive an overwhelming sense of peace.
This I believe to be a certain and infallible sign that we have made the right decision.
This is a universe of peace and harmony.
Man alone has dislocated it. When we are in God's will we are in harmony with the universe.
Peace is one of the fruits of the spirit. (Galatians 5:22)
If God said to me, "I will give you any gift you choose. What will it be?" my answer would be simply,
"Lord, give me peace."
We can face the darkest nights of the soul when we have God's assuring peace.

Kenneth W. Krueger[10]

Litany

Come to me, all you who are weary and greatly burdened.
O Lord, I need your rest.

Take my yoke upon you and learn of me.
O Lord, I need your gentleness.

My yoke is easy, and my burden is light.
O Lord, I need your strength.

My yoke fits well, will you wear it?
O Lord, I accept your will.

Benediction

Lord Jesus, Bearer of our burdens, Comforter of the sorrowful, we would bring to thee all whose hearts are sad. Help us to mediate thy strengthening sympathy to others, but grant that we may be so continually refreshed by our companionship with thee that we may not be crushed by the world's burdens. Thou art the burden bearer—not we. Thou alone, O Christ, canst in thy strong heart carry the woes of the world. In this faith, teach us to do our duty day by day as we see it to be thy will, and save us from the depression of those who try to carry more than they were made to bear and ever look to thee, O Lamb of God, who bearest the sins of the world. Amen.

---

10. Kenneth W. Krueger, *How Can I Know the Will of God?* (Nashville: Discipleship Resources, 1976), 9.

CHAPTER
SIX

DOING GOD'S WILL

[By Rebecca Laird]

Armchair travelers love to learn about exotic locations. Many can recite amazing details about the countries to which they have traveled in their minds while reading books or leafing through the pictorial wonders in *National Geographic*. Yet, actual travel in distant places is much more challenging than reading about such an adventure. Traveling is hard work that demands making numerous decisions and navigating through unfamiliar territory.

Likewise, we can spend weeks understanding and talking excitedly and wistfully about the will of God as if it were a far-off land without ever applying the insights to the struggles and spiritual terrain of our everyday lives.

Doing the will of God takes courage, fortitude, and discipline. For these we must pray. And as we seek, pray, and then act on what we know of the will of God, we can rest assured that we will be at peace, much like the bird on the wing that travels with seeming effortlessness, because both the bird and we are doing that for which we were lovingly created.

Remember God's Will for You

When life's questions and dilemmas lead you to ask yourself, "What is God's will for me?" recall that God's will is directly related to God's original and everlasting intention for you. The intentional will of God is evidenced in the ways in which God pours himself out in goodness. In Genesis we read that God created humankind in the divine image and declared that everything in creation was "very good." There in the garden a harmony existed between God, Adam and Eve, and the natural world. That was God's intention in creation. This remains God's intentional will today. God wants good to befall us. When the circumstances of life and the sufferings of our sinful world disrupt God's intention, we need to remind ourselves of God's kind desires toward us. God does not inflict illness nor strike down innocent people through tragedy. The natural laws of the created universe have consequences when disregarded, and we experience suffering as a result of transgressions against the natural order, and admittedly from many other mysteries of life that we do not fully understand.

In times of dire circumstances we can curse God or accept that we are subject to the divinely ordered natural laws of the universe. Our task is not to get mired in asking "why?" but to actively respond to evil, positively and creatively, so as to wrest good out of evil circumstances. By so doing we open up the way to God's ultimate triumph. Thus, we can cooperate with God's circumstantial will that promises to finally redeem us from suffering and tragedy. We can remain steadfast in our conviction that God is the author of good, and act rightly even in the face of grave difficulties until God's outpouring of goodness can once again be seen and felt.

Job, the man in the Bible who lost family, fortune, health, and friendship, kept the faith when nothing else pointed to God's goodness. Even after his inexplicable losses, he humbly said, "I know that you can do all things and that no purpose of yours can be thwarted" (Job 42:2). Job was affirming God's ultimate will: that harmony and communion be established between God and humankind, and that goodness prevail. We believe and trust that God's ultimate will shall one day be fully realized.

Learn to Discern God's Will

Sometimes when we seek God's will for a particular problem or situation in life, we act as if all we can do is lick our index finger, lift it high in the air, and hope that we can feel which way the wind is blowing. Thankfully, God graciously has given us more than whimsy to depend on when discerning God's will. We have been designed for a relationship with God, and those who know God are the quickest and surest at discerning God's will. We cultivate friendship with God and discern God's will by listening to *conscience*, the inner voice that tells us what is right from what is wrong; *common sense*, the God-given ability to judge a situation through thoughtful assessment; *wise advice*, the insight of a friend who stands outside the emotional setting of our particular problems; *scripture and great literature*, the accounts of how God has led and upheld great men and women who have come before us; *the church*, the collective counsel of loving Christian people, both past and present; and *the inner light*, the knowledge that comes directly from God during prayer, meditation or soul searching. It is the "voice" of God that is heard in one's heart.

It is important to remember that God usually speaks through a medley of these. God's will is discerned through listening by all of these means (and others, such as the disciplines of fasting, study, active service, and worship). What we hear in our hearts will not contradict the inspired spirit of the scriptures. The voice of God is one voice, although we may hear it in myriad ways. Discerning God's will for major decisions may take some time. Our first impulse may or may not be in sync with God's will. As Proverbs 3:6 reminds us "In all your ways acknowledge him, and he will make straight your paths."

Ours is to seek, God's is to direct. And when we discern God's will, ours is to act; God will grant us courage and strength enough to do what we must. Ours is to believe and God's is to bring ultimate triumph in all and through all things.

CHAPTER SIX
WORKBOOK

DOING GOD'S WILL—Living by God's Plan.

Purpose of the Lesson

To summarize how to understand the will of God.

A Prayer Before You Begin

Loving and gracious God, I step forward today to do your will. Be present to me and grant me the courage that I need to keep moving onward. Amen.

Key Scripture

"We have not ceased praying for you and asking that you may be filled with the knowledge of God's will in all spiritual wisdom and understanding, so that you may lead lives worthy of the Lord, fully pleasing to him, as you bear fruit in every good work and as you grow in the knowledge of God. May you be made strong with all the strength that comes from his glorious power, and may you be prepared to endure everything with patience, while joyfully giving thanks to the Father, who has enabled you to share in the inheritance of the saints in the light" (Colossians 1:9*b*-12).

Scripture Background

The Letter of Paul to the Colossians was written to a Gentile church that was being influenced by heretical teaching. Knowledge of God was being presented as an intellectual matter that was available only to a few and required strict adherence to dietary laws and ritual observances. Paul emphasizes that Jesus has already freed those who believe and that knowledge of God's will results in fruitfulness and personal maturity. In this particular passage, Paul is praying that the Colossian believers understand the great truths of Christianity and apply them to everyday decisions and tasks, for knowledge of God's will must be translated into our lives.

Key Concepts

• Doing the will of God takes courage, fortitude and discipline, and for these we must pray. As we seek, pray, and then act on what we know of the will of God, we can rest assured that we will be at peace, much like the bird on the wing that flies with seeming effortlessness because it is doing that for which it was lovingly created.

- God wants good to befall us. When the circumstances of life and the sufferings of our sinful world disrupt God's intention, we need to remind ourselves of God's kind desires toward us.

- We can remain steadfast in our conviction that God is the author of good, and so act rightly even in the face of grave difficulties until God's outpouring of goodness can once again be seen and felt.

- When we discern God's will, ours is to act, God's is to give us courage and strength enough to do what we must.

In the space below, write out the details of a problem or difficulty that you or an individual in your family is facing. Then consider the questions that follow.

CASE STUDY #1

Considerations

1. What is the good that God wills for me or for this one for whom I care?

2. How can I cooperate with God's will in these circumstances to bring good out of this problem or pain?

3. Write a prayer for yourself or for the one whom you love. Reread Colossians 1:9b-12 if you need inspiration.

In the space below write out the details of a relationship problem that you or an individual in your family is facing. Then consider the questions that follow.

CASE STUDY #2

Considerations

1. What is the good that God wills for all of those involved?

2. How can I cooperate with God's will in these circumstances to bring good out of this problem or pain?

3. Write a prayer for this relationship. When you are through consider whether it would be helpful to share this prayer with those involved.

In the space below, write out the details of a church or small group problem that your congregation is facing. Then consider the questions that follow.

CASE STUDY #3

Considerations

1. What is the good that God wills for all those involved?

2. How can I cooperate with God's will in these circumstances to bring good out of this problem or pain?

3. Write a prayer for your church. Read Acts 2:42-47 as a reminder of what the church at its best is like. When you are through, consider whether it would be helpful to share this prayer with your minister or other church leaders.

Exercises

1. Today at breakfast or during a morning break, pray the prayer you wrote for your individual need for guidance. At lunch pray the prayer you wrote in response to a relational need. At dinnertime pray the prayer you wrote for a church-related problem.

2. Describe the kind of attitude you wish to have in the midst of your present circumstances.

3. Compile a list and post the specific acts you can do to cooperate with God in bringing good out of the problems you face. Set aside some time for prayer, phone calls you could make, tasks you could perform, advice you could seek out, and so forth, and act upon each of the items on your list.

4. Write a prayer of thanks to God for what you have learned during the past few weeks about God's will for your life.

Worship Resources

Reading for Reflection

Do not stint or measure your obedience or your service. Let your heart and your hand be as free to serve Him as His heart and hand were to serve you. Let Him have all there is of your body, soul, mind, spirit, time, talents, voice, everything. Lay your whole life open before Him, that He may control it. Say to Him each day, "Lord, enable me to regulate this day so as to please Thee! Give me spiritual insight to discover what is Thy will in all the relations of my life. Guide me as to my pursuits, my friendships, my reading, my dress, my Christian work." Do not let there be a day nor an hour in which you are not consciously doing His will and following Him wholly.

Hannah Whital Smith[11]

Litany

May you be filled with the knowledge of God's will in all spiritual wisdom and understanding.
Lord, hear my prayer.

May you lead a life that is fully pleasing to God.
Lord, hear my prayer.

May you bear fruit in every good work as you grow in the knowledge of God.
Lord, hear my prayer.

May you be made strong with all the strength that comes from God's glorious power.
Lord, hear my prayer.

May you be prepared to endure everything with patience.
Lord, hear my prayer.

May you give thanks to God who has enabled you to share in the inheritance of light.
Lord, hear my prayer.

Amen.

Benediction

As a bird in flight, we ask that you, O God, enable us to do your will this week with seeming effortlessness, as we act upon the things for which you have so lovingly strengthened and created us to do. Amen.

---

11. Hannah Whitall Smith, *The Christian's Secret of a Happy Life* (New York: Ballantine Books), 178.